The Laws
of
Hell

T0096762

IRH PRESS

BOOKS
IRH PRESS
New York

ISBN 13: 978-1-958655-04-7
ISBN 10: 1-958655-04-X
Cover Image: Ma ry/Shutterstock.com

Printed in Canada

First Edition

The Laws of Hell

"IT" follows.....

Ryuho Okawa

IRH Press

Contents

Preface 19

CHAPTER ONE

Introduction to Hell
Teaching Modern People about Hell

1 Familiarizing Yourself with Hell 22

2 The Danger of Distorting the Religious Truth by Worldly
Logic

Suppression of the freedom of religion by the president of
a religiously affiliated university 26

The wrong decision-making due to a religion founded on
hellish reasons and political pressure 31

Religion must be independent from worldly logic, common
sense, and power to preserve its Truth 33

3   How the Spiritual Truth Has Historically Been Denied
    by the Established Powers

Religious people and writers who were persecuted or
politically taken advantage of 36

a) Christians who were persecuted to abandon faith 36

b) Manichaeism—its founder was flayed alive and killed, and
the religion was driven to extinction 37

c) How the reincarnation of Jesus is exiled in Dostoevsky's
novel 38

d) Tolstoy escaped persecution by depicting a non-spiritual
Jesus 39

e) Confucianism was used as a Godless and soulless teaching
to rule the country 40

Christian and Buddhist teachings about wealth were distorted
in later years 42

a) The danger in taking the issue of "good and evil" to the
extreme 44

4   Why No One Can Teach about Heaven and Hell

The knowledge modern people should have: Souls and the
idea of reincarnation 47

Advancements in natural sciences led to materialistic and
atheistic Buddhist studies and philosophy 51

5   What Separates Heaven and Hell according to Buddha

The true meaning of the teaching: "A stone sinks in water,
but oil floats" 55

The mistakes of ancestral services and chanting, as seen from
Buddha's teachings 57

a) Problems with religious groups that focus only on
ancestral services while discarding spiritual discipline 57

b) Misleading teachings of the Nichiren School and the True
Pure Land School of Buddhism 58

Acts of salvation can sometimes be invalid, as seen in the
story *The Spider's Thread* 62

6   How Will Your Sins Be Judged after Death?

All of your wrongdoings will be shown in the
Life-Reflecting Mirror in the afterlife 67

People who believe in materialism often end up becoming
earthbound spirits 71

CHAPTER TWO

The Laws of Hell

The Judgment by Yama That Awaits You after Death

1   **Yama's Thinking That People Today Should Know**

In principle, those without faith will fall to hell 74

Faithless and ignorant religious professionals will end up
in hell 76

The court of Yama has the records of every thought, action,
and inner voice you had while alive 79

2   **The Sin of Ideological Criminals Is Heavy**

Wrong speech will be given a harsh verdict 84

New types of hell: Newspaper Hell, TV Hell, Weekly
Magazine Hell, and Internet Hell 85

Yama's agency will never forgive influential ideological
criminals 88

3   **Worldly Values Are Not Valid in Hell**

Spiritual discipline in this world is worth 10 times that in
the Spirit World 92

Ideological criminals are isolated in the Abysmal Hell 95

4 The Rule of Hell and the Various Aspects of Hell

Legitimate wars are not considered crime but hellish ones
will lead to the Asura Hell 98

Materialistic pleasure-seekers arrive at the Hells of the
Bloody Pond, Mountain of Needles, and Forest of Razor
Leaves 102

5 Physical Pleasure and the Price to Be Paid in the Afterlife

Self-control distinguishes humans from animals 105

Cherish your physical body as a "holy temple" for the soul
to reside 108

Human rights in this world are not considered in hell 110

6 Your Faith, Thoughts, and Actions Will Certainly Be
Judged after Death 114

CHAPTER THREE

Curses, Spells, and Possession

How to Control Your Mind So You Do Not Fall to Hell

1   Curses, Spells, and Possession Lead You to Hell

Are you going to heaven or hell? —It depends on how you live now 118

The difference between a curse and a spell 120

The examples of spells I received from other religious groups 122

Case 1: A deadly spell cast by a religious group based in Tachikawa City 123

Case 2: A spell cast by an esoteric Buddhist sect in Kyoto 125

Your mind will be tuned to hell if it constantly emits negative vibrations 127

2   The Three Poisons of the Mind That Are Tuned to Hell:
    Greed, Anger, and Foolishness

Greed: Japanese folktales warn of excessive desire 130

Greed and the urge to do evil as seen among former and
prospective students of prestigious schools 132

Anger: What to do when you are raging with anger from not
being able to win 134

If opportunity does not arise, another path will open up 136

Foolishness: Not knowing Buddha's Truth invites
ignorance 139

a) Ignorance of translating Confucian teachings superficially
by removing the dignified tone 141

b) The mistake in the interpretation by the Tendai School
and the True Pure Land School of Buddhism 143

Scholars who are ignorant of the Truth will go to hell even
if they are not evil in a worldly sense 147

3   Pride, Doubt, and False Views Lead to Curses, Spells,
    and Possession

Problems of having pride and doubt 151

a) The mistake of doubting and denying Buddha's teachings
and his biography from the perspective of modern medical
knowledge 152

b) The mistake of doubting and denying all mystical
phenomena in Buddhist scriptures from the perspective of
biology 154

False views: Ideas that have deviated from the Truth will lead
to curses, spells, possession, and hell 158

4 How to Prevent Yourself from Falling to Hell

You will know which hell you will go to by simply
reflecting on your life 161

Make an effort to turn your mind into a mirror and wipe off
bad thoughts 162

CHAPTER FOUR

The Fight against Devils

Revealing the Reality of Devils and Their Tactics

1   Historically, Religions Have Fought against Devils

Devils target those with strong influential power 166

How devils in hell came into being 169

The Christian ideas of purgatory and hell show how small-
minded human beings can be 170

Hell and devils that were born as a result of the wars
between Christianity and Islam 175

2   The Deepest Pits of Hell You Never Knew

Sixteen major hells that await materialists after death 177

The types of people who fall straight to the Abysmal Hell 180

The sin of Nietzsche: Criticizing Christianity with
Übermensch theory 183

In Japan, vengeful spirits are enshrined to prevent them
from cursing people 185

3   Even Now, Devils Haunt Certain Religions

The danger of psychic-power worship lying in evil psychic
religions 190

The difference in "guidance" between the spirits in heaven
and the devils in hell 193

The problems of the Unification Church 196

In both religion and politics, you need the right purpose,
motive, means, process, and results 202

The mistaken thinking of "adverse destinies will naturally
break away, and good results will follow" 204

4   Fighting against Devils Also Requires Using Worldly
    Common Sense and the Law of Causality 207

CHAPTER FIVE

A Message from Savior

Saving the Earth from Crisis

1 Earth Is in the Greatest Crisis in History

The COVID scare among humanity and the dangers of an
imminent major war 210

What would happen if the law becomes "God"and takes
control 212

2 We Must Not Allow Earth to Become Devils' Planet

This world is being allowed to exist as a school for soul
training 216

The danger that the system of reincarnation might stop 218

The "world emperor" might appear and annihilate ethnicities
and nations that believe in God or Buddha 222

3 Begin the Spiritual Fight to Regain Human Nature

Establishing El Cantare Belief all over the world in this
modern age 226

Explore Right Mind and practice the modern Fourfold Path ... 228

1) Love—Make a paradigm shift from "taking love" to
"giving love" 229

2) Wisdom—Study Buddha's Truth to develop your soul 230

3) Self-reflection—Look back on your thoughts and actions,
the sins you committed, and polish your mind 231

4) Progress—Create utopia where those who have
accumulated virtue can lead many people 232

Strive to create a better society by practicing the Fourfold
Path 234

4　My Hope Is to Maintain Earth as the Training Ground for Souls

Utopia on earth—The world of *Truth*, *Goodness*, and *Beauty* ... 236

Each of you must accomplish your grand mission—Save the mind of each person 237

Afterword 241

About the Author 247

What Is El Cantare? 248

Books by Ryuho Okawa 250

Happy Science's English Sutra 258

Music by Ryuho Okawa 259

About Happy Science 260

Contact Information 262

About IRH Press USA 264

Preface

A terrifying book is finally complete and ready for you.

Never did I imagine that *The Laws of Hell* would be published in this 21st century world—this convenient and affluent world that is, at times, dominated by fear of a nuclear war or a coronavirus pandemic.

Who can write such a book in this modern age?

There is only one person, here, in a small oriental country, Japan.

This is his 3,100th book.

That's Him—yes, the One who lives in the same age as you yet has been sent from what would seem like an infinitely distant world to you. He was once called Alpha and also Elohim.

The Laws of Hell is another form of the laws of salvation. "Did you read *this* book or not?"—You will soon be asked at the entrance to another world.

Ryuho Okawa
Master & CEO of Happy Science Group
November 2022

CHAPTER ONE

Introduction to Hell

—Teaching Modern People about Hell

1

Familiarizing Yourself with Hell

Across several lectures, I would like to talk about hell. To begin with, I will focus on giving you an introduction to it in this chapter.

Until today, I have been giving lectures on various topics. However, as the number of lectures increases, more people lose sight of what is most important and find it difficult to fully grasp them. But at the least, I would like the majority of people today to learn about the existence of hell. I want people to know how close hell is to them and be familiar with its existence. In a broad sense, the teachings on hell are also the laws of salvation that will save people.

The only chance that people nowadays have to learn about hell is mainly through horror movies, but they do not necessarily accord with Buddha's Truth. In a way, through horror movies, fear has been turned into a form of entertainment. So it can be said that the people working in this "fear industry" are making money by entertaining people.

Therefore, I do not necessarily think that these people are the enlightened ones who are trying to guide people in the right direction. There are countless horror movies, and although they could be considered a mixture of good and bad, I scarcely find any good ones. Too many of them can be categorized as a pile of junk.

These people can make such horror movies because many of them already have a hellish mindset. Therefore, they can relate to that world and are always full of ideas to make such movies.

Although people can portray hellish phenomena, the issue here is that no one can give an answer as to how we should deal with them. People today have become extremely weak at this. In old stories, for example, you would see Buddhist monks sending lost souls to heaven or Taoist masters fighting to exorcise devils. There are also stories of people being saved by virtue of Buddha and God or by the power of a sutra. Today, however, people no longer believe or are interested in the spiritual virtue depicted in these stories. This is a dire situation.

I am especially concerned about the work of temples, shrines, and churches. At least these places should teach their believers, maybe every Sunday, about God or Buddha. They should preach, for example, "Souls really do exist, and so do heaven and hell. That is why you should not live in so and so way; instead, you should live in this way," or "If you are living in a such-and-such way, please reflect on yourself." If they are giving these kinds of sermons to help people repent on themselves or to provide people with the opportunity to reflect on themselves every week, they are fulfilling their role as a religion. But it is a shame that there are hardly any that do so. I sometimes find that some are doing exactly the opposite of what they really should do. This is very disappointing.

Take Buddhist monks, for example; you need professional qualifications to become one. But as I have mentioned a few times before, some authorized Buddhist universities in Japan that produce monks seem to be teaching that Buddhism is atheism. Some even teach that Buddhism is materialism.

If they are calling it atheism because Buddhism is about Buddha and not God, it is still tolerable because it is a matter of naming. But if they go as far as to say, "Buddhism is atheism and materialism," then that is almost no different from Marxist communism.

Even if people, after completing a specialized course at a Buddhist university, get officially certified and are assigned to a temple as a chief monk—just like a doctor starting his own medical practice—this certification would be meaningless if it is based on the wrong knowledge. People usually think that any Buddhist university can make you a monk, but if what they are teaching is materialism, then there is a problem.

The same goes for philosophy. It was originally similar to religion, and the two have the same root. But "clever" people liked to twist and complicate the logic, and they gradually made it more and more abstract and theoretical. It is no longer about philosophical thinking now. Instead, it is almost becoming a part of mathematics. It seems that philosophers are also mathematicians, and parts of philosophy have become the study of symbolic logic. Such philosophy has absolutely no power of salvation—almost zero. Just as there are heretical and evil ideas in religions, wrong ideas have been expanding in the world of philosophy too. This is indeed unfortunate.

2

The Danger of Distorting
the Religious Truth by Worldly Logic

Suppression of the freedom of religion
by the president of a religiously affiliated university

Among existing religions, there are groups that were founded by a leader who was spiritually possessed by a devil or, in other words, founded on a hellish reason. This is also problematic.

There are also religious groups that have worked too closely with political power and have become its tool. This would not be an issue if what they are doing is out of righteousness, but oftentimes it is wrong. God or Buddha is sometimes used to threaten and govern people because worldly power alone is not enough for political leaders; we must be cautious of this. I can only feel sorry for the people who believe in such religion even today.

In the past, we sent an application to Japan's Ministry of Education, Culture, Sports, Science, and Technology (MEXT) to establish Happy Science University (HSU), but the government just tossed the case over to the council and had them do the decision-making. This is their way of avoiding responsibility. Politicians often avoid responsibility by passing down difficult issues and leaving them in the hands of academic experts.

The first time we applied, the council chair was the president of a Christian university. He had only written one book, but for some reason, places like the Chinese government had given him many awards, such as honorary doctorates and medals. I could see that he was completely tamed by China and had already become a tool of communism. The same is happening in some Christian universities. Our political party is fighting against communism, so the Chinese government has also been manipulating these people to retaliate against us.

Such a person was assigned to lead the council that reviewed our application. When I heard that he had received many honorary doctorates and other awards from China and South Korea, I thought we got bad luck. I presumed that he believed that religions are acceptable only when protecting established authorities but are unacceptable if they threaten them. Given that he had assimilated communist ways of thinking, it was obvious that he would deny any spiritual phenomena.

Usually, the council must screen the application and make a decision based on the submitted documentation that describes the purpose of establishing a university. But they disapproved the establishment of HSU for a reason other than what was written in the documentation. For example, Happy Science publishes spiritual messages. Even though this had nothing to do with the application, they concluded, "This religion publishes spiritual messages. So it is not academic. That is why we cannot approve HSU as a university." Frankly, this is nothing but a breach of the constitution. (Another possible reason for disapproval was that the Liberal Democratic Party of Japan at that time had an intimate relationship with the former Unification Church.)

Many religions receive spiritual messages and revelations from God, Buddha, high spirits, and angels, or they experience spiritual phenomena. As long as there is freedom of religion, the government cannot rule out a religion by saying, "A religion that experiences spiritual phenomena is not real." That is obviously religious oppression. So the council's reasoning for disapproval was clearly wrong. Yet these actions are left unpunished.

What is more, spiritual phenomena and what is commonly called spiritual fraud are completely different things. Spiritual phenomena are the universal grounds for the emergence and existence of religion as a whole.

The decision by the MEXT was wrong in terms of both the constitution and the law. The approval of universities must be made as legal judgment based on the screening of documentation, but they rejected HSU based on something other than what was written in the documentation—which is the very religious activities of Happy Science. They have practically decided that religions other than the established or acknowledged ones are all fake.

However, HSU is under the umbrella of Happy Science, which is a religious corporation that the ministry had approved. Logically, they are completely contradicting themselves. It seemed that the decision was based on whether the political administration ruling at the time could take political advantage. If they could, they would positively consider the application, but should there be any political disadvantage, they would not.

Thus, they disapproved HSU by saying that we publish spiritual messages. They probably made this excuse because this kind of reasoning would be well accepted by the mass media.

In addition, they said, "We cannot approve your university because, in your economics curriculum, you list a lot of professors who advocate the tax cut theory." But, of course, academic freedom applies to economics, too. Under the constitutional law of academic freedom, you can have professors who advocate tax cuts as well as those advocating tax hikes.

In general, heavy and oppressive taxation will devastate people's minds and ruin the country. In Japan, during the Edo period (1603–1867), riots usually occurred when people were required to pay more than half their yearly harvest as land tax. Nowadays, the government collects de facto taxes in all kinds of forms without calling it "tax." They levy taxes under the pretext of various reasons, such as pension and insurance. If these are taken into consideration, the government is already taxing around 50 percent of people's income. Even so, Japan has an enormous budget deficit that has piled up, and the government must correct its habit of being in debt. They must start by cutting costs and avoiding wasting money. Citizens must also work diligently and pay appropriate taxes, and the government must make sure it spends the tax money in the right way. We need to change our society into a healthy one in this way.

Let us go back to the tax cut theory. If the study of it leads to reexamining any waste of money, it has enough meaning. In reality, when the United States conducted tax cuts under President Reagan and President Trump, their economy improved and tax revenue virtually increased. Therefore, you cannot claim that the tax cut theory is academically wrong.

Disapproving the ideas of this theory is merely due to the public officials' selfish reasoning. More taxes mean more power for government officials and politicians, so that is why they oppose tax cuts. But if they judge good and bad, or real and fake, solely based on their self-interests, they are making a grave mistake.

The wrong decision-making due to a religion founded on hellish reasons and political pressure

I have described how I felt about the council the first time we applied to establish our university. The second time we applied, the council members were different; the new council chair was a former president of a university affiliated with a different Christian sect (the Church of England). He had studied a subject similar to political philosophy during his university days. He published, like the previous council chair, only one book. It was the research on Rousseau, which was an extended version of the research paper he wrote when he was an assistant researcher. The Christian church his university was based on was founded in the Middle Ages.

From our religious understanding, the church was established for the wrong reasons. It was started by a king who wanted to escape the control of the Roman Catholic Church; he parted from it by appointing himself the supreme head. Because the Catholic Church interfered with the king's marriage and divorce, he created a new religion by becoming a priest himself. He was the type of person who would think of killing his wife if he could not divorce her, and he actually killed many others. This was the historical background of the founding of this religion.

The new council chair used to be the president of a university based on this sect of Christianity, and he studied Rousseau for his academic research. It is commonly said that all those who have researched Rousseau end up being leftists.

Rousseau had five children without getting married, and he sent them all to an orphanage. This was the man who wrote about idealistic education in *Emile, or On Education*.

Many admirers of Rousseau developed their own educational ideas based on his. But I do not think a man who had five children, abandoned their education and care, and threw them all into an orphanage is qualified to teach about education in the first place. Of course, there are either well-behaved or ill-behaved children, and once they become adults, they have to be responsible for their lives. Even so, since Rousseau left all his children in an orphanage while they were still young, he is not worthy of teaching about education.

So the council chair was the kind of person who did research on such an irresponsible man and was a former president of a university affiliated with the Christian church founded on a hellish reason (its founder Henry VIII is now a devil in hell). This kind of person screened our application.

In the process, we were even given political pressure. The ministry pressured us by suggesting that we should withdraw the application rather than be rejected. So we decided to withdraw it for now and reconsider it. In this way, power relations and worldly matters prevent us from purely pursuing righteousness. We cannot stand being judged by those who are on the wrong side.

Religion must be independent from worldly logic, common sense, and power to preserve its Truth

If the things that are prevailing, popular, or established are fixed and are wrong, then there is not much we can do. At this level, all we can do is stand on our own feet and walk the path we believe in.

Political powers are now putting pressure on us by not awarding degrees to the graduates of HSU. Nevertheless, its graduates have become staff of Happy Science or are hired as university graduates by companies that are related to or are supporters of Happy Science. It seems that over 98 percent of the students have been hired as "university graduates."

This means we are *independent*.

If we are not independent, we will have no choice but to distort our basic teachings as a religion and even the content of our activities. This is dangerous, and as a religion, we must not give in on this point.

We must not be defeated by worldly logic and the established common sense of this world.

Nowadays, people use the word *democracy*. The U.S. president, for example, is currently working under the banner of spreading democracy to the rest of the world. But North Korea also thinks of themselves as a democratic country. Even China thinks of themselves as a democratic country. So just advocating "democracy" will not justify themselves. What must be considered next is the content of their "democracy."

For example, China promised Hong Kong that they would maintain the same system for 50 years after the handover, but China began to completely disregard their promise after just 25 years. Publicly, they are making it look as if they are maintaining the system, but only "patriots" are allowed to run for legislative elections. In this case, a patriot means a member or supporter of the communist party. Therefore, people who oppose the Chinese Communist Party cannot become politicians, and this is the same as having no political freedom. There is neither the freedom to run for an election nor the freedom to vote. Their "democracy" is a mere formality. This is one example.

In democracy, there are "democracy with faith" and "democracy without faith."

Thus, it has become difficult to understand religious truth in this world, and at times people's sense of values has flipped upside-down. Religions often experience hardships in this world because people with worldly power or higher status can put considerable pressure on or make judgment calls on them.

3

How the Spiritual Truth Has Historically Been Denied by the Established Powers

Religious people and writers who were persecuted or politically taken advantage of

Many major religions of today have also experienced persecution in the past. This is because religions that work to change people's fundamental sense of values will always clash with the existing or established powers.

a) Christians who were persecuted to abandon faith

Historically, there have been religious groups that have been acknowledged and adopted by authorities within 50 years or so at the earliest, but even Christianity went through 200–300 years of persecution.

For a few hundred years, Christians continued to suffer— they were crucified, sometimes upside down, and stoned to death. At the Roman Colosseum, Christians, not gladiators, were chased and eaten by lions and made into a show. They were forced to choose to either abandon their faith and be forgiven or keep their faith and be eaten by lions. There were times when they went through this kind of persecution.

God did not come down to save them at those moments. So it was indeed very harsh. But people were tested to see whether they could keep their faith to the end, despite all the hardships they had to endure.

As a result of persecution, some religions survived, whereas others disappeared.

b) Manichaeism—its founder was flayed alive and killed, and the religion was driven to extinction

Another example is Manichaeism, which spread and became a world religion while the founder was still alive. But after the founder was flayed alive and killed, the religion was driven to extinction.

You would think that Manichaeism was persecuted by Christianity because it was founded later. But we know it was Zoroastrianism that put Mani to the death penalty. In fact, our spiritual research has revealed that Mani's past life was Zoroaster. Such things can happen; you could be killed by the very religion you had created in your past life.

c) How the reincarnation of Jesus is exiled in Dostoevsky's novel

In the Christian world, too, there is a prophecy that says if Jesus were to be reincarnated, he would be persecuted.

I sometimes refer to "The Grand Inquisitor" from *The Brothers Karamazov*. In the 16th century, a man thought to be the reincarnation of Jesus appears, heals the sick, and does various miraculous deeds as Jesus did. The Grand Inquisitor himself knows that the man is the reincarnation of Jesus, but he says something along the lines of, "We don't want you to come back. Now that the church system has already been established, there is no place for you. We don't need you." In other words, the church system was already taken over by the devil, and they exiled the man by saying, "We can execute you because you are interfering with the devil's work. But instead of doing so, we will commute your sentence and have you exiled."

There is indeed a 99 percent chance that this will happen. I have partly included a similar episode in my novel, *The Unknown Stigma 1 <The Mystery>*. It depicts a saint—Sister Agnes—who appears in this modern world and performs miracles as Jesus did. The Christian church does not want to acknowledge her powers, so it tries to prove that she has demonic powers. Agnes escapes from the church out of fear of persecution. I valued such a prophecy and novel of the past and included it in my novel.

d) Tolstoy escaped persecution by depicting a non-spiritual Jesus

Dostoevsky wrote *The Brothers Karamazov*; around the same time, there was another famous writer named Tolstoy.

Tolstoy wrote *The Gospel in Brief*. In the book, he did not include any description of mystical phenomena and depicted Jesus as a mere moral person. Tolstoy probably thought that people would find it easier to accept, given their level of awareness. So he wrote about Christianity in such a way to teach morals.

This is rather a disappointing work compared with the original Bible. But for his literature to be recognized and for him to earn his living under the regime at the time, he

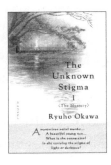

The Unknown Stigma 1 <The Mystery>
(New York: IRH Press, 2022)

probably had no choice but to omit the descriptions of miracles and other mystical phenomena to that extent. He probably worked it out and thought that his work would be accepted and he would not be persecuted if he wrote about Christianity as moral teachings.

Regardless, some people apparently protested or opposed what he did. One source says that Umeko Tsuda, who studied in the United States during the Meiji period in the 19th century and returned to Japan after studying Christianity, truly despised Tolstoy. On reading his gospel and seeing that all miraculous phenomena had been omitted, she perhaps thought, "What a coward!" I won't speak any further because I do not know the details, but maybe there is such a way of thinking.

e) Confucianism was used as a Godless and soulless teaching to rule the country

Another example is Confucius. Confucius, who taught Confucianism, continues to influence China for over 2,500 years, but sure enough, his teachings on attaining success in life were gradually taken advantage of by the political regime. Confucius once said, "I shall not talk about things like supernatural powers or mysterious gods." The regime took these words out of proportion and overly emphasized them to promote atheism.

At another time, Confucius was asked about the afterlife. There is a part in *The Analects* where he says something like, "How can I talk about what happens after death when I have not yet fully understood human life and what it means to live?" The rulers of the time just picked out certain lines and used them to promote Godless and soulless ideas.

What is more, the rulers skillfully used Confucius' political ideas to make those in lower positions pay the utmost respect to those above them and prioritize loyalty. They took advantage of these ideas and used them to rule the country. That is why they used to hold the imperial examination based on *The Four Books and Five Classics*, which are said to be mainly taught by Confucius. This is the same as what China is doing now—excluding anyone from the government who is not a "patriot."

For more than 1,000 years, the imperial examination system, which could be considered the bar examination or the civil service examination, continued. Furthermore, you had to obtain a near-perfect score to pass the exam that tested you on an ideology that was convenient to the ruling authorities. But even if you get a high score on this test and are labeled a prodigy, it does not mean you are living in accordance with the Truth. In fact, the authorities just hire the people worth using for their advantage.

Even if religious ideas are taught, in many cases, the authorities only use the parts that are convenient for them while leaving out the inconvenient parts. Although religion and politics share some common values, they also contradict each other. This is a very difficult matter.

Christian and Buddhist teachings about wealth were distorted in later years

Religion and economics also share some common principles, but there are aspects that contradict each other.

The reason Protestantism grew popular compared with Catholicism is that the rise of Protestantism coincided with the rise of capitalism. They taught that becoming successful in business, earning great profits, and achieving prosperity in this world meant realizing the glory of God on earth. They also upheld the theory of predestination, which said that whether a person is saved is predestined. It means if a person diligently worked and grew very rich in this world, they are blessed by God, and that is why they prosper. In this way, Protestantism affirms wealth.

On the other hand, Catholics have some kind of "allergy" to money, and they are not so keen on making money. You can certainly find such a description in the Bible: "It is easier for a camel to pass through the eye of a needle than for a rich person to enter the kingdom of God."

If you just extract these words, you can turn this teaching into communist thinking.

Many kinds of teachings were given because of the various circumstances of the given age and were taught especially for the situations of the time. But each teaching was preached to a specific person or a group of people. So although the above teaching certainly applies to the rich with greedy minds, it does not always apply to the rest.

It also depended on Jesus' standing at the time. If he was a leader of an already established large group, he might have taught differently. But he gave the teachings when Christianity was still a new religion that had just emerged. For example, when a very rich man who had never done wrong came to Jesus, he was told, "Go, sell what you possess and give to the poor." Upon hearing that, he went away in sorrow, thinking he would not be able to keep up with such a religion. However, Jesus gave the teachings on a one-on-one basis, especially for the individual. I am sure he would have taught different things to different people. This teaching was not tailored for everyone.

Even though Judea back then was practically a Roman colony already, rabbis—Jewish teachers—and other very rich Jewish people had high social status. Because of this, protecting the pre-existing authority was important for them at the time. That is why they resisted any idea that could overthrow their power. Disciples in later generations cannot understand this historical background.

There is a similar example in Buddhism as well. One day, Shakyamuni Buddha and his disciple were walking along a mountain trail, and they saw a gold coin on the ground. Buddha then said, "Be wary. A poisonous snake is waiting with its mouth open." He said this as a warning because monks might neglect their discipline and become corrupt if they started picking up coins off the ground. This teaching remains, but if those words were used out of context, it would simply mean, "Money is dirty."

That is why, in Hinayana Buddhism, monks are not supposed to directly receive money with their bare hands. Some groups teach their monks that when receiving offerings, they must spread a cloth such as a handkerchief or blanket on the ground and have people place the money on it before wrapping it up, as they believe touching money would defile them. However, in truth, they have fallen into the trap of formality.

a) The danger in taking the issue of "good and evil" to the extreme

These ideas of good and evil are a matter of a general endangerment offense. For example, if you drive a car, you can get into an accident and kill someone or yourself. This can indeed happen. But there is something wrong if you go as far as to say, "That's why people should never ride a car."

In Japan, there was a time when about 10,000 people—or more—died from traffic accidents per year. This number has now reduced to around a few thousand. We have gotten used to this number, so we do not make it an issue, but what if someone suddenly brings it up and says, "Thousands of people die because cars are sold. Should people be making money from that?" It may sound as though automobile companies are selling deadly weapons.

Even when viruses spread, the annual number of death in Japan was a few thousand or not even 10,000. They might get infected but do not die easily from it. On the other hand, if we assume that more than 10,000 people definitely die from car accidents every year, how many people have died ever since cars came into existence? The answer amounts to a significant number—perhaps over a million.

In the end, it is a matter of how you think. You could think of a car as a deadly weapon or a lethal vehicle, but this aspect cannot outweigh its convenience. You would not need a car if trains were running everywhere, but some places do not have them. You cannot travel everywhere by boat, and even if you want to use an airplane, sometimes the airports are too far. So although there is a risk of getting into an accident, it is convenient to have a car. That is why there is scarcely any protest to get rid of cars even if people could die from car accidents; they just depend on insurance to cover them.

To reduce road accidents, considerable improvements have been made, for example, from driving techniques to traffic safety; simply having a mirror at an intersection can prevent you from hitting an oncoming car; having headlights on at night can prevent you from getting into an accident; just setting rules to drive on the right or left side of the road prevents accidents; something as simple as properly following the rules at an intersection can reduce accidents. These kinds of efforts are being made.

As you can see, there are difficult aspects regarding the issue of good and evil.

4

Why No One Can Teach
about Heaven and Hell

The knowledge modern people should have:
Souls and the idea of reincarnation

If the teachings of early Buddhism were literally applied to the world today, then taking the life of any living creature, for example, would be considered wrong. When Shakyamuni Buddha was alive, hunters who caught birds and animals in the mountains and fishermen who caught fish in rivers and seas were considered to be engaged in impure professions. For this reason, they were not allowed to become renunciant disciples or sometimes even lay believers. It was unfortunate for them, but this shows that Buddhism started off with a very strict attitude.

This custom still remains to this day. Actually, it may not have started from Buddhism; it was most likely inherited from Brahmanism, which preceded Buddhism in India.

In the West, people believe that only humans have souls, so they do not feel any remorse about killing and eating animals. Whether they be pigs, cows, or birds, people do not believe that animals have souls, so they have no qualms about killing and cutting up the meat and eating it. In the East, on the other hand, there is a belief that animals, too, have souls. Some people take this belief very seriously.

In Japan, beef curry has become a national dish popular among adults and children. But if an Indian person is invited to Japan and eats it without knowing what is inside, then as soon as he learns there was beef in the curry he ate, it may trigger something in him, and he may possibly die from shock.

In India, cows are believed to be God's messengers, so people do not kill them. Even cars will avoid them if they are crouching in the middle of the road. That is why cows in India have peaceful and heavenly facial expressions. They have gentle eyes, too. If they knew they would be eaten, their sadness would show on their faces, but because these cows know they will never be eaten, their expressions are gentle.

In some respect, however, this is one of the factors that delay modernization. If cars stop because of the crouching cows, it would be problematic during rush hour.

When you go around India and eat curry, the only meat you are served is tandoori chicken. It seems to be fine to eat chicken but not any other kind of meat. So, other than that, you can only get beans or vegetable curry, which may not be satisfying for Japanese people.

I presume this is not an idea original to Buddhism. It existed before Buddhism, and the idea of reincarnation underlies this belief. The idea of reincarnation originally says, "Those who lived a life unworthy of humans or lived like beasts or animals will be reborn as animals in their next life." Such an idea has streamed into Buddhism, and Buddhism does not deny this idea itself.

In India, you would see large black carp-like fish swimming in the river. So you would wonder why people do not catch and eat them if there is a food shortage, but Indians would say, "They might be my grandpa or grandma, so I cannot." This is also a difficult part.

Even so, the Western belief that "animals do not have souls" is actually wrong. Sheep have souls and so do cows; therefore, the belief is clearly wrong. Westerners think that way because Jesus did not teach whether animals have souls or not.

If you look at the philosophy of Plato—which he wrote as Socrates' idea—that came a couple of hundred years before Jesus, you can find descriptions of how humans are sometimes reborn as animals. These descriptions are written in some of his philosophical works. For example, a person who lived a courageous life in this world will be reborn as a lion, or a person who wants to prove their innocence will be reborn as a swan. Such descriptions can be found, which means that ancient people shared similar ideas of reincarnation. Even though this idea was included in philosophy, Jesus could not preach it during his three years of missionary work.

In the area Jesus lived, there was a custom of writing words with blood. Maybe this served as a seal or stamp. People there extracted sheep blood for writing words and killed sheep or goats for food during festivals or when welcoming someone.

I am not sure of the exact difference between sheep and goats. Apparently, sheep live in the plains, whereas goats live in the mountains, so they are a little different. Anyway, people killed and ate them. This was not considered a sin, although, of course, stealing them was considered a violation of property rights and, therefore, a sin. This kind of traditional custom has blurred the truth.

Based on the spiritual research I conducted now in the 21st century, if I were asked in a straightforward manner: "Are people sometimes born as animals?" or "Are animals sometimes born as humans?" I would have to answer, "Yes." Nevertheless, its percentage is not very high; it does not happen to just anyone. It comes as an option when that is considered the best choice for a person. So I must admit this happens in reality. I want you to know this fact about reincarnation, though many people nowadays think of it as folklore.

Advancements in natural sciences led to materialistic and atheistic Buddhist studies and philosophy

Some Buddhist scholars, including great scholars of the post-WWII period, believe that the idea of humans being reborn as animals is just silly ancient folklore or a parable to scare and teach people morals. Maybe this was also partly because pre-WWII Buddhist scholars from the Meiji period onward adopted Western philosophy. What is worse, they did not stop there and took it one step further: some have gone as far as to say, "Humans don't have souls," or "Buddhism teaches soullessness. It puts forth a theory of atheism and soullessness." Like so, they believe this is the modernization of Buddhism.

However, I would like to tell them, "Hold on a second." I think these scholars say those things by extracting only a part of the teachings, but if their ideas were true, Buddhism would be considerably similar to what Marx advocated as communism. That is, "There is no God or souls, so the only important thing is happiness in this world. Everyone should be treated the same and equally to achieve this happiness, even if it means distributing the earnings people have gained through work. That's the way to be happy."

Philosophers tend to think this way. They believe that once you have faith, you will believe in just about anything, like how the Japanese proverb goes: "A human being can even have faith in a chopped sardine head (if you have faith, even trivial things will appear sacred)." They believe that faith will prevent people from thinking philosophically.

Science has adopted a stance that you need to doubt, doubt, and doubt everything, and the truth lies only in what you cannot doubt. If the same kind of stance is adopted in the study of philosophy, some professors might as well tell you to abandon faith. This was actually depicted in the American movie titled *God's Not Dead*. It became quite a hit. I remember the movie was based on a true story: a student with religious faith won a debate with his professor.

In the movie, a philosophy professor tells his students to sign a declaration denying God; that is the requirement to take his class. But one student refuses by saying, "I'm a Christian, so I cannot." The professor warns the student that he will not be able to pass the required course with an "A." Not getting an "A" would work against him when finding a good job or taking a certification exam. So even his girlfriend, whom he has a stable relationship with, leaves him. She tells him to sign the paper, but because he does not, she leaves him. She probably thought she could not marry such an "idiot." She says something like, "Just sign the paper. You can't afford to flunk this class if you want to join the elite track." However, he hesitates because, as a Christian, it goes against his faith. Then, he gradually gains more and more support until the professor finally leaves the classroom in defeat.

Perhaps the movie was popular partly because it dealt with a rare case. Nonetheless, this is a difficult issue. I presume the same thing is most probably happening in the field of philosophy in Japan as well.

The natural sciences have advanced and are developing based on materialism. This makes it seem as though religious studies, Buddhist studies, and philosophy are rather outdated and superstitious. That is why people specializing in those fields are also trying hard to lean toward materialism.

Looking at the current situation, we have now reached the point where no one can actually teach about heaven and hell.

Even among the teachings of Shakyamuni Buddha, some parts can be misinterpreted as atheism and materialism. For example, a Buddhist scholar named Hajime Nakamura published *Kamigami to no Taiwa* (Japanese translation of Samyutta Nikaya Part 1 or Buddha's dialogues with gods) and *Akuma to no Taiwa* (Japanese translation of Samyutta Nikaya Part 2 or Buddha's dialogues with the devil) by Iwanami Pocket Edition. These original scriptures were not about denying gods. They describe how the ancient gods of Brahmanism were awestruck by the power of Shakyamuni Buddha after speaking with him. They were so moved that they walked around Buddha clockwise several times to express their worship.

The scriptures do not deny gods; rather, they pass on how Buddha's authority was established after debating with the gods that are equivalent to the ethnic gods in ancient Japan. However, because this story can be misinterpreted as denying the absolute power of gods, some people pick up that point and say, "Buddhism is atheism."

5

What Separates Heaven and Hell according to Buddha

The true meaning of the teaching: "A stone sinks in water, but oil floats"

There is a Buddhist sutra called Sutta Nipata, which is believed to be a relatively accurate record of Buddha's words. It is compiled in the Agama Sutra. It archives the story of Buddha's confrontations with the pre-existing religions.

Back then, Brahmanism, which eventually became known as Hinduism after the establishment of Buddhism, had already incorporated fire-worshiping rituals that came from Zoroastrianism in the West. This practice of fire-worshiping rituals is now found in some schools of Buddhism; some esoteric Buddhist groups make a bonfire by stacking wood in the shape of a tic-tac-toe grid. So perhaps I should not deny this practice too much. Fire does have a purifying effect and can symbolize burning up the sins of this world. Since before Buddha's time, there has been a teaching that says, "If you make a bonfire and pray for the well-being of your ancestors, your sins will be forgiven."

To counter this idea, Buddha put forward a new, innovative teaching. Of course, he did not deny everything about fire worship, but he said, "Whether you will go to heaven or hell depends on your mind and action. It depends on your thoughts and actions."

Action means *karma*. What you have thought and done in this world will shape your karma, and this karma will determine your next life—this is the basic teaching of Buddhism.

So it is your thoughts and actions that determine whether you go to heaven or hell. This is expressed in a parable in the Agama Sutra: "Here is a pond. What if you throw a stone in it? The relative density of a stone is greater than that of water, so it will naturally sink to the bottom. Now, will the stone float up if the Brahmins pray for it? No, it won't."

The parable is talking about people's karma or, in this case, their sins. It teaches that you cannot be saved if you fall to hell because of your heavy sins. It is your own responsibility.

The parable then continues: "On the contrary, if you throw a pot of oil into the pond and you pray to your ancestors so that the oil will sink to the bottom of the pond, will it sink? No, it won't. The oil will surely float to the surface." This means the oil has a smaller relative density than water.

In short, the parable teaches that those whose sins are light will naturally float above the water, which means they will go to heaven, whereas those whose sins are heavy, like a stone, will naturally sink to the bottom. In other words, you will not be saved by just making a bonfire or praying to your ancestors. It is not an almighty teaching, but in a way, it covers the essential point. Almost all of the new religious groups of today that are misguided are mistaken regarding this point.

The mistakes of ancestral services and chanting, as seen from Buddha's teachings

a) Problems with religious groups that focus only on ancestral services while discarding spiritual discipline

I will not mention his name, but a famous Japanese author, who was also a politician, believed in a certain religion. Apparently, he had received over a million votes from those who were affiliated with this group.

The group heavily focuses on ancestral services. (I wonder if people are aware that this group—Reiyukai [literally, Spiritual Friendship Association]—is a misguided religion.) I do not think an ancestral service itself is bad. But this religion just blames your ancestors for your misfortune by saying things like, "Many bad things are happening to you, and your business isn't going well because your ancestors are still lost." They say that your ancestors are the reason why your family does not get along with each other or why they died from illness or accidents. They put all the blame on ancestors in this way and conclude that all you need to do is conduct ancestral services, and there is no need for spiritual discipline.

I am not saying that the ancestral service is bad, but if you think that you will be saved by just doing that, then you are wrong. That is because you are not held responsible at all for your thoughts and actions with this way of thinking. However, this group continues to say, "Conduct more ancestral services."

b) Misleading teachings of the Nichiren School and the True Pure Land School of Buddhism

There are many sects in the Nichiren School of Buddhism. I cannot make a sweeping statement because some of them may correctly understand Buddha's teachings, whereas others may not. But some groups say, "Whatever happens, be it conflict, bankruptcy, or murder, or whatever the trouble may be, just chant '*Namu-myoho-renge-kyo* (devoting one's life to the Lotus Sutra).' Just chanting it will save you from everything." However, because it would be too easy to just chant, some people say, "Your chanting is not enough. Chant it one million times."

It is quite a discipline to chant *Namu-myoho-renge-kyo* one million times. It takes great energy and effort to chant it one million times while keeping track of the number of times you have already done it. In this way, the religion makes the believers think that chanting will solve all their problems. However, I have to say this teaching contains some lies.

"Namu" in *Namu-myoho-renge-kyo* means "to pledge devotion," and "Hokke-kyo" or "Ho-renge-kyo" means the Lotus Sutra. So *Namu-myoho-renge-kyo* means "I pledge devotion to the Lotus Sutra."

The main message of the Lotus Sutra is Buddha's teaching: "This world is ugly and dirty, like the pit of a swamp or mud. But from such a filthy environment, a lotus grows its stem straight up. Even in the muddy pond, a lotus grows its stem and blooms a truly heavenly, beautiful white flower above the surface of the water. It lets an innocent flower bloom."

Namu-myoho-renge-kyo summarizes the teaching like so: "Even as you live in this corrupt and dirty world, keep your mind pure and let your lotus flower bloom magnificently." This is what the phrase is saying, and there is no mistake in chanting *"Namu-myoho-renge-kyo"* if you have this understanding.

> This world is like a muddy pond, a marsh, or a swamp.
> We are in such a corrupt world.
> Know it. See it.
> Look, we are in a world of suffering.
> Look, we are in a world of sadness.
> But even in such a world,
> We can make a lotus flower bloom.
> That is the practice of Buddhism.
> You must always bear this in mind as you live.
> That is what it means
> To pledge devotion to the Right Teachings.

Once you understand this, you will know how you should live. This world is full of temptations that lead you to various evils or make you corrupt. However, do not be absorbed by them. Let a pure white flower bloom. Let a magnificent lotus flower bloom. That is the goal of your life.

In a sense, this chanting phrase *Namu-myoho-renge-kyo* summarizes the essence of Buddhism well. If this is your level of understanding, then there is no problem chanting it.

Other groups that belong to the True Pure Land School of Buddhism chant *Namu-Amida-Butsu* (Namo Amitabha

Buddha) instead of *Namu-myoho-renge-kyo*. As I said, "Namo (Namu)" means "to pledge devotion," so this chanting means, "I pledge my devotion to Amitabha Buddha."

Amitabha Buddha is the Buddha that saves—the aspect that emphasizes Shakyamuni Buddha's salvation and mercy. By being embraced by Amitabha, you become one with Him through abandoning everything of yourself. You devote yourself and your life to Amitabha and become one. So you concentrate your will on Amitabha while becoming one with His Will.

The original meaning of *nen'butsu* is not just to verbally recite "Namo Amitabha Buddha." It means to contemplate (nen) Buddha (butsu). In other words, it means to picture Buddha in your mind and contemplate Buddha. However, because this is a difficult thing to do, many religious groups have a *gohonzon* (a sacred item that represents the object of faith) to represent Buddha. It is usually a statue or painting of Buddha or something else. You receive a *gohonzon* as a substitute and pray to become one with Buddha by tuning the vibration of your mind to the *gohonzon*.

You pray in your mind, "I'm a person with many sins, but I entrust everything to Buddha. I will leave it to Your Will," and become one with Buddha. In meditation, you vividly visualize Buddha in your mind, wishing to become one with Buddha. By doing so, you hope for your peaceful death and rebirth in the land of Perfect Bliss.

This idea itself is not wrong. However, it will be wrong if you misuse it and emphasize it too much, saying, "Whatever crime you may commit, you will be saved by just chanting *Namo Amitabha Buddha*," or "You will be saved by just thinking, '*Namo Amitabha Buddha*.'"

Suppose a man wearing a clown mask with a machine gun, like the Joker, the archenemy of Batman, commits many crimes, such as robbing banks, killing many people, or setting fire to the pile of money he has stolen. Imagine if people think, "There's no problem because he can be saved by chanting *Namo Amitabha Buddha*." Obviously, this is wrong. If *Namo Amitabha Buddha* is misused to encourage people to commit crimes, this religious teaching is indeed wrong.

Acts of salvation can sometimes be invalid, as seen in the story *The Spider's Thread*

When a person who committed many sins can reset his mind by completely changing his attitude, then this is called a *conversion*.

You instantaneously direct your mind toward Buddha and aspire to be a person who can be embraced by the great mercy of Buddha. You strive to live your life in the right way from now on and believe in Buddha. Every day, you visualize Buddha in your mind. This is the meaning of nen'butsu.

So think about Buddha and live in tune with Buddha's Will. Do not live in a way you will feel ashamed of when seen by Buddha.

When you experience conversion, instantaneously change your mind, and enter the right path, a saving hand will reach out to you. This ought to happen; it is not wrong.

But, of course, there are exceptions. For example, there is a short story, *The Spider's Thread*, by Ryunosuke Akutagawa. It magnificently portrays an element of the Truth.

In the story, Shakyamuni Buddha—although he should actually be Amitabha Buddha—is walking around the lotus pond in heaven. He looks down into the pond and sees all the way down to the bottom. This is a metaphor explaining in an easy-to-understand way that a great tathagata can see what is happening in the lower worlds using his clairvoyance.

Buddha looks down into the pond and sees hell. In the Hell of Lust, otherwise known as the Hell of the Bloody Pond, he finds a man named Kandata drowning in the sea of blood and suffering. Many other lost spirits are also suffering there.

In the eyes of Buddha—who is, in a way, omniscient and omnipotent—the kind of person you are is obvious; in just a glance, he can spiritually see through all your lives, including your past lives.

Despite how bad of a person Kandata was and the many evildoings he committed, Buddha saw how he did one good thing during his lifetime—that is, Kandata saw a spider while walking on the street one day and felt sorry for it, so he let it go when he could have stepped on it.

Buddha thinks, "Kandata did one good deed. He was a complete villain, but he once showed compassion for a living creature. He had a touch of mercy. He shall be offered salvation on this single point." So Buddha lowers a spider's thread down from the lotus pond in heaven to save Kandata from the Hell of the Bloody Pond.

A spider's thread is a perfect description. This exquisite expression is very much the style of Akutagawa. It is indeed a thin, fragile piece of thread that looks like it would break at any point. Such a thread is smoothly lowered down until it hangs in front of Kandata, who is drowning in hell.

"Oh, a spider's thread came down," thinks Kandata, and he grabs hold of it. He thinks it might break, but because the thread is as sturdy as a fishing line, he starts to climb it.

Up and up, he keeps on climbing. He climbs even more desperately as he thinks, "I can escape to heaven if I go higher up." But when he glances down for a moment, he sees other spirits crawling up from below, one after another.

Sadly, Kandata does not have enough faith. He thinks a single spider's thread can only save Kandata himself. Spider-Man saves his friends and girlfriend with his thread, so Spider-Man's thread can save a person, indeed. But Kandata can hardly believe that such a thin, unreliable thread could carry that many spirits. He thinks, "If it breaks, that will be the end for me. This spider's thread is mine."

Kandata may have a point. But the moment he shouts, "You guys, get your hands off! Or else it will break!" the spider's thread snaps just above his hands, making him and everyone fall right back into the Hell of the Bloody Pond. Then, as if nothing happened, Buddha goes back to strolling around the lotus pond, and soon it is noon.

As a writer, Akutagawa had an amazing talent to be able to summarize this Truth in a simple, short story. I assume Akutagawa could understand the heart of Shakyamuni Buddha to some extent.

Thus, it is not enough to just have moments of faith and want to enter the right path. If you strongly wish to only save yourself and think, "I don't care what happens to other people. As long as I'm saved, it's good," then the helping hand will become "invalid."

Let us say you drew a fortune slip at a shrine or temple, and you got "great blessing." Then, you might think, "Oh, I'm glad I got 'great blessing.' But only I should have it, and other people should not be drawing it." You are determined that there should not be any more fortune slips with "great blessing," so you enter the shrine or temple, open up every fortune slip, and rewrite all the "great blessing" marks with "future blessing" or "small blessing." In this way, you preserve the "great blessing" fortune slip only for yourself.

Just imagine a person like this. Isn't such a person shameful? Some may think, "I can't stand others becoming happy. Only I should be happy," but people with this kind of thinking are so egocentric that they are not worth being saved. You may agree.

The more good you do, the lighter your sins become. But if you become too competitive and selfish to the point that you put down other people or get rid of them so that you alone can be happy, then your chance to be saved will be "invalid." Your will to seek the Truth or your converted mind will be meaningless. Please know this. This is a fundamental point.

As I said earlier, this is the general rule: a stone sinks to the bottom of the pond, whereas oil floats to the surface. In other words, if you have lived with good thoughts and good actions, you will naturally go to heaven. However, if you have committed crimes or lived with many bad thoughts and actions, you will sink to the "bottom of the pond."

6

How Will Your Sins Be Judged after Death?

All of your wrongdoings will be shown in the Life-Reflecting Mirror in the afterlife

One of the reasons heaven and hell exist is to prevent people from escaping the meshes or the rules of the Spirit World, even though they may have managed to escape the meshes of the law of this world and think they have had the last laugh.

In this world, some people commit murder and are sentenced to death, life imprisonment, or 20 years in prison, for example. Such people, who have atoned for their crimes while they are alive, will have their sins slightly reduced. They may not be completely exempt from further punishment, but their sins will be slightly lessened.

On the other hand, others commit murder in this world without getting caught. Such people may be thinking, "I got away with it. What a relief. I managed to keep my honorable career status to the end." However, Yama[1], also called Enma in Japanese, who is the Special Judge of Hell, definitely exists in the other world, and he will reveal all their sinful deeds.

Since ancient times, there has been a Life-Reflecting Mirror. Nowadays, it might be like a movie screen or a television screen or on DVD rather than a mirror. It shows the key topics of your life, one after another. You will watch it for yourself and have no choice but to reflect on your life. Then, based on the "evidence," you will be asked, "What do *you* think of a person like this?"

During the screening, your relatives, friends, and others who passed away before you will also be present, like the jury, and they will give their opinions too. Your life will be shown until you can accept it and think, "Well, I guess I have to go to hell." Then, a "hell tour" starts. This is what will happen to you. So, even if you manage to slip through the meshes of the law of this world, such as the criminal code, you cannot get away.

Even if you believe in heaven and hell, perhaps you think only criminal offenders will go to hell. Or you might be thinking that, in addition to criminal offenders, people who broke the civil code, such as those who refused to pay off their numerous debts and ran away, might go to hell. Nevertheless, some laws in this world are wrong; there are even laws that were only made to favor certain political parties to win elections. For this reason, you cannot say that all of the laws are right.

People are apt to think that those who live by the law are good people, whereas those who do not are bad people. We can say that this is true in general. But we are not sure if the laws in China or North Korea, for example, are even right; in that case, there is room for consideration. Nevertheless, the wrongdoings that were not judged by the laws of this world will be judged in the other world.

Symbolically, there are beings known as Enma-sama or King Yama and punishers (ogres). People used to think red and blue ogres only appeared in old tales, but our recent spiritual messages from the "Red Punisher" prove that they exist in reality—they are real entities. They most likely look like red or blue ogres in the eyes of the sinners, but they probably seem completely different to others. The punishers may look like prosecutors, whereas King Yama may look like a judge. In places like hell, the world looks different based on the person's mind. What you see may not be what it really is, but what is certain is that a verdict will be made.

The "hell tour" also exists. Various hells exist in great numbers, each corresponding to the sin that was committed. You will go around them one by one.

Now, even in the 2000s, I have been saying that this is true. There is virtually no one who can say this today, so I must tell this myself.

It is important to have faith, but of course, that alone is not everything. Faith is important in that it helps you to head in the right direction, but it does not mean, "As long as you have faith, you can all go to heaven."

But this is what Christianity generally teaches. They say, "If you have Christian faith, you will go to heaven. If you don't have Christian faith, you will go to hell." On hearing this, people started questioning, "If that's the case, what about the people who came before Christianity? Will they not be saved?" To solve this issue, Christianity introduced the idea of "purgatory."

Purgatory is the same as what Japanese people generally think of as "hell." In Japan, people believe that souls in hell can return to heaven if they have deeply reflected on themselves and atoned for their sins. Thus, the hell that people think of in Japan is, for the most part, equivalent to purgatory. On the other hand, Christian churches refer to "purgatory" as a place from where souls can return to heaven after they repent, and "hell" is referred to as a world from where souls can never ascend.

In fact, this latter type of hell truly exists. Souls who have become devils are least likely to come up to heaven. Those who have become devils or fallen to the Abysmal Hell—a place that can be likened to the bottom of the deepest well—will not be able to get out so easily. Ideological criminals who led many people astray cannot come out. There are such cases, and this is the knowledge I want you to have.

People who believe in materialism often end up becoming earthbound spirits

There is much more to be said about the different aspects of hell, and I cannot talk about all of them here. However, I would like to add a new point.

Many of you might think, "When people die, they leave this world and go to a completely different space— either heaven or hell." But today, materialistic and scientific thinking is widely prevalent, and the education system teaches this, so a tremendous number of people believe that the other world does not exist. For those who do not believe in the other world, there is neither hell nor heaven. That is why they do not have any place to go after they die. Because they have nowhere to go, this third dimensional world, known as the Phenomenal World, is the only place they can reside. They can neither recognize hell nor heaven, so they continue to stay in this world.

These souls believe they are still living in this third dimensional world. They think, "People just can't hear my voice," "I don't know why, but I can pass through walls," "For some reason, I don't seem to bump into people but pass through them," or "I'm now in a mysterious world, but I'm probably ill or hallucinating." There are many such souls, and their number is increasing tremendously.

We can say this is also a type of hell.

So hell does not exist separately from this world. Souls that have been judged as evil are in hell, but those who are unaware of their own death and stay in this world are also in a type of hell. Please understand it this way. There are actually many souls like this—very many, indeed.

Some of them become earthbound spirits and haunt places such as hotels, schools, or railroad crossings where they committed suicide. Others might possess the person who ran them over in a car accident. Like so, there are many spirits committing many evildoings. This is hell in this world. How they are living is the same as being in hell. You must know this.

In this chapter, "Introduction to Hell," I presented an overview of hell. I believe I must go into further detail on its specific teachings.

CHAPTER TWO

The Laws of Hell

—The Judgment by Yama That
Awaits You after Death

1

Yama's Thinking That People Today Should Know

In principle, those without faith will fall to hell

This lecture, titled "The Laws of Hell," is probably one of the important chapters of this book. The title, "The Laws of Hell," may sound too broad and difficult, but to put it in other words, it is what Yama is thinking about. I want to talk about something that will truly be of help to you, which is the reality of how you will be judged after death.

In general, this world takes on the principle of legality, where the law indicates the kind of punishment you will be given for certain actions you take. Then, those who violated it would usually become criminals. However, because people in the world today have not only lost their faith but do not study the religious Truth and lack morality, there may hardly be anyone who will want to listen to things like, "If you do this, you will go to hell."

To the majority of people today, hell is perhaps the negative incidents that they experience in this world. For example, when they go through worldly misfortunes such as losing their job, becoming heartbroken, suffering from violence, or being killed, they call it "hell" or feel as though they were "caught up in a hellish situation."

However, the truth is that everyone is destined to die. There is no exception to this. In the modern age, you may live up to 120 years at best, but you cannot escape death; anyone who is born will definitely die. No matter how advanced medical science becomes, it cannot defeat death—100 percent. Although it is possible to delay people's death or temporarily improve their condition, it is impossible to make a human being that never dies. The only way there could be immortal humans would be to create something like everlasting robots, but even robots eventually break down, run out of fuel, or face other issues and go out of use.

The vast majority of animals have a shorter life span than humans, so we are likely to come across the death of animals, including pets such as dogs and cats, during our lifetime. We also see the death of other animals that become our food. To cite a familiar example, even the kids who catch and collect insects such as rhinoceros beetles or stag beetles during summer come to understand the simple meaning of death by witnessing them die.

So what should you do or how should you think? The first essential point is this: Those without faith will, in principle, fall to hell.

By faith, I am not specifically talking about belonging to a particular sect of a particular religion. People with faith could be, for example, those who truly believe in the existence of God or Buddha, high spirits, Angels of light, and bodhisattvas, regardless of whether they can clearly express it in words.

They could also be those who think, "Perhaps people who committed wrongdoings will go to hell. The appropriate way of living for humans is to do good things, and it is preferable for good people to live happily in the other world." When the verdict is made to decide whether one should go to heaven or hell, those without such religious beliefs basically fall to hell.

Faithless and ignorant religious professionals will end up in hell

We are entering an age when people depend on worldly ways to solve everything. This is causing problems.

For example, some people think that the reciting of a sutra is all about sound. Today, there are agencies that record a skilled monk's recitation of a sutra, program it into robots, and then dispatch them to funerals in place of monks. They provide such services, and the price apparently varies depending on the length of the sutra. They charge, for instance, ¥200,000 (about US$1,400) for an hour and tell their customers: "It will cost you between one and two million yen (about US$7,000–14,000) to hire a real monk, or perhaps even three or four million yen. Our service is more affordable." They think of themselves as a discount store and are working like a service business.

However, all those that are involved in creating this new service—this includes the developers of the robots, the salespersons of these robots, the service providers, as well as the customers receiving the service—I will have them all go to hell. I definitely will not forgive them. The people working in this kind of business are giving in to materialistic values in the world to survive; that is by ignoring the spiritual world and the essence of Buddha's Truth, and turning religious services into worldly tasks. But I will never allow this. Reciting a sutra is different from a musician singing a song, so it must not be treated in the same way.

There is virtuous merit when a sutra is recited by someone who understands the essence of it; the dead will be sent to heaven, or a guiding angel or bodhisattva may come while the sutra is being recited. But if it is recited by someone, even a professional monk, who does not understand the sutra at all, then their recitation will not be effective. If these monks neither believe in the other world nor the virtuous merit of the sutra, nor understand its content, and are just carrying out their work like any normal job, then they are no different from inept doctors. Even monks will essentially go to hell if they are faithless, tell lies, or deceive people.

The same is true for the pastors and priests of churches. Some are faithless; nevertheless, they take over a church as a family business to make a living and support their family. Pastors are allowed to get married and have children because they need children to take over their profession, but not everyone who takes on the profession has faith. Some just graduate from a divinity school as a mere custom and learn about God so that they can keep a roof over their heads. Unfortunately, these "professionals" who make a career out of religion without knowing its essence will go to hell. I will not forgive them.

In reality, such "religious workers" are also active in hell because many souls there want to be saved. Again, these religious workers preach false doctrines and teachings in hell and confuse those souls, thus prolonging their stay in hell rather than saving them. In principle, I will not forgive them. They will be met with harsher consequences. If they continue to lead many people astray even after going to hell, they will fall even deeper into an even more painful world.

Therefore, first, you will be severely judged on whether or not you have faith or you have some kind of belief or state of mind that may not exactly be faith, but similar.

The court of Yama has the records of every thought, action, and inner voice you had while alive

Next, you will be made to look back on your life as a human being, and your thoughts and actions will be examined. Actions are relatively easier to judge than thoughts. The laws and regulations in this world determine what you must not do, such as crimes and illegal acts. So it is quite obvious.

However, there are other wrongdoings that many people do while thinking, "It's all right as long as no one notices." Nevertheless, even these acts that people thought they got away with without anyone finding out will all be exposed after death. Their lives will be shown on a Life-Reflecting Mirror or as a "video clip" of their life events, and they will be told on which points they have to reflect and be made to repent over the things that they have done.

But it is not just wrongdoings that will be judged. In the court of Yama, both the good and bad deeds will be reviewed. They will be compared, and a verdict will be made based on the weight of the two.

Therefore, even people who committed murder may be given a certain degree of allowance if they were sentenced sufficiently on earth and were able to rehabilitate during their long imprisonment or if they worked diligently to start their lives over after returning to society. The same is true for executed criminals. In most cases, they will not be able to return to heaven at once, but if they repent on their life and realize that they had failed as human beings, they will go to a place like a self-reflection facility to receive guidance to look back and reflect on themselves for a certain period of time. Once that period is over, they can go up to heaven.

In other cases, however, the Special Judge of Hell will never overlook people who act and think, "It's fine because no one knows what I did." These are people who committed murder, assault, or injury without being noticed, those who acted behind the scenes and did not get caught, or those who committed robberies, thefts, and other criminal acts and escaped without being arrested by the police or tried under the law. There are also smart criminals who skillfully used other people to carry out the crime, pretended to have nothing to do with them, and never got caught. Yama will *never* let such people get away.

In this world, a person cannot be convicted without evidence, but in the court of Yama, all evidence will be spiritually shown because everything you did and thought during your life as a human being is recorded. As you watch the records, you will notice that they are mostly taken from the perspective of your guardian spirit. Some of them are taken from the perspective of your own eyes, but the fact that you can see yourself on the screen means that there was someone observing you from a third-party standpoint. So you can assume that, in general, each person's guardian spirit films and records that person's life. And these records even include your inner voice.

You will be shown a shortened version of this record and must review your entire life through it. In this way, evidence will be presented to you in the other world. In this world, you may not be convicted without the information collected from police legwork, a testimony of the witnesses, or your own confession. Sometimes, the forensics team must find some scientific evidence to prove you are guilty.

In the other world, however, all evidence will be presented in front of you. Even if you forget the various things that you did as you grew older, you will recall every single thing when you return to the other world.

There, the metric of time is quite different from how the clock ticks in this world. You may have heard about mountain climbers falling off and getting flashbacks of their entire life in a matter of a few seconds before hitting the ground. It is like that. You will be shown not the entire 60 years of your life on earth but only a series of important points that need to be examined. In this way, your entire life will be examined in an extremely short period of time.

Thus, the trial of the Special Judge of Hell conducted before people are sent to hell is fair. Every single thing that people think and do in this world has been recorded without exception.

These records also exist within your own soul. In the past, I have used the term "thought tape" to describe it; it is like a tape recorder. All your inner voices and the actions you took are recorded as if they were filmed, so anyone who can read the thought tape will be able to immediately tell what kind of person you are.

Vinyl records were popular in the past; you had to play the record and listen to the music for an entire hour to tell what kind of music it was. But according to the laws of the other world, we can instantly tell the "type of tune" one has by simply looking at the grooves on his or her "vinyl record." In particular, spirits at higher levels, or high spirits, can instantly read it and tell how a person has lived their life.

If the person being judged is still unconvinced of their verdict, then their deceased acquaintances, such as their friends, relatives, or victims may be spiritually invited. If the acquaintance of the "defendant" is still alive, then the person's guardian spirit may be summoned as a witness. They might be asked, "This is what he is saying. Is it true?" Such investigation will be conducted.

Let us say that a person defaulted on his rent for many years and killed his landlady because he was repeatedly asked to pay for it, like in the novel *Crime and Punishment*. Even if the police investigation could not find the murderer, Yama can summon the spirit of the landlady and have her come face-to-face with the murderer. Then, Yama can ask, "What really happened?" And the landlady's spirit might respond, "Yes, this person killed me. I'm sure it was him." In that case, the evidence is clear. The murderer will then be shown a clip of the crime scene as well.

So you cannot get away with doing bad things.

What is the important point here? In reality, as a human being, it is difficult to live without doing anything bad. Life is a workbook of problems to be solved. In this sense, doing bad things means that you made mistakes in solving the problems. Mistakes do happen. But the important thing is to get a passing score. You might lose some points, but you must aim to increase the points you gain and get a passing score in life.

Do you think you are living rightly when viewed in light of right faith, the law of this world, or human morals? What would your parents think? What would your neighbors think? What would your coworkers think? What would someone with a higher awareness think? Please consider these points.

2

The Sin of Ideological Criminals Is Heavy

Wrong speech will be given a harsh verdict

The judgments made for crime in this world contain many mistakes. For instance, some weekly gossip magazines may believe they are playing the role of Yama in this world. Based on this belief, they try to hunt down people's wrongdoings.

Some of their articles have a point, so their sentence could be mitigated, but they also publish wrong articles. They may think they are acting like Yama, but if they continue to demean or hurt people or corner them to lose their jobs with fake stories, they will fall to hell. Over 90 percent of editors-in-chief of weekly magazines, as well as directors and those responsible for deciding which stories to cover on television programs or in newspapers, have now gone to hell.

Today, democracy is built upon public opinion, but it is a "flawed democracy" if public opinion itself is wrong. This is why the population of hell is now tremendously increasing. It is truly troublesome. What is more, in many cases, it is nearly impossible to convince people of their mistakes after they have gone to hell, so we are having trouble.

They are indoctrinated with the wrong thoughts because those with the authority to make judgments in this world are wrong.

I do not think many university professors commit crimes in this world; however, if they teach wrong ideas, their students will be "contaminated," and this "contamination" will continue to spread to later generations. These professors are called "ideological criminals," and their sin is more serious than you might imagine. Various crimes in this world, such as murder and robbery, are easy to identify, but it is more difficult to identify ideological crimes.

Although the Japanese Constitution advocates the freedom of thought and the freedom of speech, should the freedom of wrong speech, in particular, be allowed? A harsh verdict will certainly be given on this point. Those who drag many people into misery or guide others in the wrong direction will naturally be held accountable.

New types of hell: Newspaper Hell, TV Hell, Weekly Magazine Hell, and Internet Hell

Today, we are living in an "internet society," where anonymous users are writing many hate comments, causing a "blow up" online. Although lawmakers are discussing it, the legislation is lagging behind in this field. This is also an urgent issue in hell that is currently under research.

There are people who make slanderous or critical comments toward others online. These people write comments that they would not say or that would be unreasonable to say face-to-face. Furthermore, they might write things that would be unacceptable to say in the presence of other people. By doing so, they demean others or set others up. Even those who used such "speech violence" in anonymity are now judged as new types of criminals.

Traditional hells alone are no longer sufficient in dealing with such crimes. To be more specific, the new types of hell that are starting to form are Newspaper Hell, TV Hell, Weekly Magazine Hell, and Internet Hell. Experts are needed for each of these hells, so the judges of these are those with some expert knowledge on related matters.

Nowadays, people not only lie or hurt other people; they commit bigger, more systematic crimes using computers. For example, hackers steal data from other companies or foreign countries and misuse it illegally. They also use computers to steal another person's assets saved in a foreign bank. These people will be caught if there is evidence, but most of the time, they are skillful and leave no traces.

Computer-related currencies have also been circulating. These currencies may be allowed if there is a sense of trust and if righteous-minded developers and operators are working to support people's economic activities based on good intentions and trust.

However, some people are simply creating a lot of cryptocurrencies as a type of fraud or using electronic money to commit various crimes. The hell for these people is unlike previous ones and is more complicated. So although I used the term Internet Hell earlier, even Cyber Hell, or rather Hell of Cyber Space, is now forming. Specialists are emerging regarding these hells as well.

Surprisingly, because many people are now working in these fields, a sufficient number of such specialists are present. So we are calling up decent and righteous-minded spirits from among them. We teach them the basic rules of the court of Yama and have them judge matters by asking them, "Based on your expertise, do you think this person did the right thing or not?"

So some spirits with skills in the STEM (science, technology, engineering, and mathematics) field are now being asked to come and help out at the court of Yama. This is because the old concepts that have been used in the past are not enough to judge the crimes of today, and some crimes are yet to be defined as crimes. These judgments need to be made.

Yama's agency will never forgive
influential ideological criminals

In this way, hell is becoming extremely complex. Previously, I mentioned thoughts and actions, and these two are linked. So first, please reflect on your thoughts on the following points.

The first is greed. Some people are very greedy, much like the greedy old couple in Japanese folktales. A greedy person would get a "red card."

Next is anger. Some people cannot control their anger and unnecessarily hurt others or give trouble to families or organizations, and they continuously create disharmony in society. In a way, such people are "polluters." The "polluters" will surely be required to clean up their mess, which means they will be made to atone for having hurt other people because of their anger.

Next is ignorance, or ways of thinking based on ignorance, as I mentioned in Chapter One. Learnings based on ignorance have already expanded enormously in the academic world too. Many people make a living by teaching junk knowledge that contains no value, and others spread it by teaching the junk elsewhere. These people will be held accountable for being ignorant. In most cases, they have chosen the wrong one out of two options. They have made the wrong decision between one and the other, or between left and right, so they will not be forgiven.

Those in the position of teaching academic knowledge must tirelessly seek the Truth, tirelessly seek Goodness, and tirelessly seek Beauty. Scholars and academic teachers who make efforts in this way have the chance of returning to the upper levels of the sixth dimensional world, but in reality, quite a few of them have fallen straight to hell. Those who continue to teach wrong ideas are "ideological criminals," even though they may have certain titles in this world, such as "Professor of XYZ University." The more they spread their philosophy and the more influence they have, the deeper hell they will fall into.

This is not only true with scholars. Many ideological criminals emerge from among commentators, writers—including novelists—and editors and directors of newspapers, TV programs, magazines, movies, and so on. The agency of the Special Judge of Hell will never overlook them, as they have wrongly influenced a great number of people. That is Yama's stance.

There are certainly "one-on-one" crimes, but this influence is rather small. Meanwhile, some people influence numerous people by sharing their wrong philosophies and ideologies through books, comics, movies, and TV programs, among other ways. Such people can be found among politicians too.

Although they may be highly regarded in a worldly sense, they will be clearly judged as "evil" under the standard of good and evil seen from Buddha's Truth.

It is essentially like pollution. If someone dumps poison or mercury in the upstream of a river, there will be abnormal fish with bent backbones. The people who eat these fish will then suffer from rare or incurable diseases, and as a result, many of their lives will be ruined. So you cannot be happy just because you have been promoted to a higher position or succeeded in this world.

On the other hand, there are those who think, "I didn't succeed in this world. My life ended up being mediocre. It was an ordinary life. I could only influence my family members, and it was a pity that my workplace treated me like a machine. It was such a boring life." But to tell you the truth, even if these people go to hell after returning to the other world, they can get out of hell rather soon because of their light sins.

However, those who made their company into a large one or made a lot of money through dishonesty will not easily be forgiven due to the magnitude of their influence. Regarding medicine, some people may have developed and sold fake medicine or promoted ineffective medicine by claiming them to be effective. These people will also be severely punished. The same is true for politicians who made wrongful laws.

Based on an earthly point of view, you might think, "Life ends in this world, so I want to be as successful as possible in my 100 or 120 years of life. I'd be more than happy if I could gain the respect of many people, make money, and be well-known. I want to be popular with the opposite sex as well." But if you had wrongful thoughts and did wrongful deeds to achieve them, please know that your sins in the next life will definitely be heavy.

3

Worldly Values Are Not Valid in Hell

Spiritual discipline in this world is worth 10 times that in the Spirit World

To put it simply, this third dimensional world is a place where it is difficult for humans to know the Truth, unlike in the Spirit World. So it makes it more difficult to do good things in this world than in the Spirit World; likewise, it is more difficult to practice self-reflection in this world than in the Spirit World.

In fact, one year of spiritual training in this world can be equivalent to 10 years of that in the Spirit World. So people who are judged as evil as a result of living mere several decades of life can suffer in hell for several hundred years. In reality, there are many such people.

There are both good and bad in this world. We are living with a physical body and are surrounded by physical objects, and we must live by making use of them. In a way, it is a world where everyone is groping their way through life blindfolded. So you will be able to make great progress in your spiritual training if you can discern good from evil, truth from falsehood, and beauty from ugliness in such a world. That is why humans are born into this world over and over again. There are many things to be learned here.

When you are in the other world as a spiritual body, it is quite easy to understand that you are a spirit. Nevertheless, many do not even understand this simple truth. The spirits who possess living people and do evil deeds have no clue about the existence of the Spirit World, and they do not understand that they are a spiritual body. Some of them believe they are still alive and possess living people to vent their feelings of frustration.

Suppose a person dies in a car accident while driving around a sharp curve on a mountain road. If the person does not know that he is a spirit, he will become an earthbound spirit hanging around that area. And when he sees someone driving recklessly or under the influence of alcohol, he will swiftly possess that person and cause another accident. Such things are really happening.

This example shows that some people do not understand the simple truth because they lack knowledge. This is unfortunate.

Several decades ago, a former prosecutor general published a semi-autobiography book titled *People Become Trash After They Die* (literal translation). This is one of the worst outcomes of materialistic thinking. Given that he was working at the top position of judging right from wrong, his sin must be heavy. He only saw things from a materialistic point of view, so although he may have believed he was walking the "road of Yama" and expected to advance straight from a prosecutor general to a "Great Yama," that is not what happened. Those with such kind of mistaken philosophies are not forgiven.

The same is true for judges. The bar exam does not test religious knowledge, so their judgment is based mostly on worldly knowledge. Thus, although the majority of their decisions—70-80 percent—may be reasonable verdicts, 20-30 percent of them are most probably wrong. Judges must ask their conscience when considering whether or not their verdicts are right. Even judges must go to hell if they have frequently handed down wrong rulings and made fatal mistakes.

Lawyers, too, must go to hell if they are immoral. For instance, some lawyers actively accuse religions of their crimes, and in some cases, they may be taking rightful actions. But if they are working to eliminate a religion that carries the mission of God and Buddha from society, then unfortunately, these lawyers will also go to hell, regardless of whether they have the title of a lawyer.

So worldly values are not valid at all in hell. Your worldly educational background and your certification do not matter. It also does not matter at all if you were respected or rich, had a large house, or had a prestigious lineage like coming from an aristocratic, royal, or noble family. None of these factors will be taken into consideration. All that matters is faith, thoughts, and actions. Your faith, thoughts, and actions will show the kind of person you are.

In a sense, it was good that aristocracy collapsed and everyone came to be treated equally. For quite some time in the past, those of higher social class were not charged with a crime, even if they bullied or killed those of a lower class. Compared with those times, the world has become better. In general, you will be judged based on whether your actions were appropriate as a human being.

Nevertheless, the laws of Yama are not just rigid rules. As I said earlier, the Special Judge of Hell weighs both the good and bad deeds of a person before determining the weight of their sin. He also considers the testimonies of the people involved and judges whether there is room for extenuating circumstances.

Ideological criminals are isolated in the Abysmal Hell

Some of the most serious offenders fall straight to the pit of hell upon death without even going through the court of Yama. They are obviously hopeless people in anyone's eyes. Among them are those who have especially obstructed or hindered others in matters related to Buddha's Truth by saying the exact opposite things. Those who were involved in activities that led to the increase in the population of hell will never be forgiven. Many of them fall to hell headfirst.

Even so, some of them stubbornly insist that there is no afterlife, God, or Buddha. In most cases, these souls are in their own illusionary world, so they might think they are locked up in a place like a special room in a hospital. However, in reality, they have fallen into the Abysmal Hell at the depths of hell.

The characteristic of the Abysmal Hell is that although there are many other souls there, they cannot see each other because of the pitch-black darkness. It is almost as if they have fallen to the bottom of a well. In terms of prison, they are in solitary confinement and are not allowed to talk to or see others. They are isolated as ideological criminals. They are in complete isolation. Even though there may be other souls within 5-10 feet of them, they can neither recognize nor speak with each other. In many cases, they are left all alone and in a state of complete isolation. As a general rule, they will be isolated for a long time.

There, some of them gradually begin to reflect on their lives. In such cases, an appropriate spirit will visit them when the opportunity arises. Just as a prison chaplain comes to see the inmates to teach them the right way of living, an appropriate spirit will visit the Abysmal Hell when the time comes. Oftentimes, the spirits that returned to heaven after death and are striving to be the light of angels will take this role. They are angels-to-be, or "angel interns." These spirits will visit hell to gain the experience of saving others and try to guide them to the right path by talking to them.

In many cases, however, the spirits in the Abysmal Hell cannot let go of the thoughts they had imprinted on their minds during the several decades of their lives on earth. These spirits are usually full of pride. They think they are very important figures, so they do not apologize to others or admit their mistakes. Thus, they suffer for a very long time in hell and cannot be saved. However, to tell the truth, they are lonely, sad, in pain, and hungry just like a prisoner serving an indefinite sentence.

4

The Rule of Hell and
the Various Aspects of Hell

Legitimate wars are not considered crime
but hellish ones will lead to the Asura Hell

At a shallower level of hell, many spirits are around. One rule of hell is that like-minded spirits gather together. In other words, those with the same "illness" are grouped in one place. Hospitals group patients with the same illness; those with mental illnesses are in the psychiatric ward, those with heart diseases or brain diseases are grouped as such, and those with cancer are placed in a cancer ward. Likewise, people with similar tendencies are often put together in the same hell. Here, they fight with other like-minded spirits and cause chaos, and by continuing to do so, they will come to realize their mistakes.

In some ages, wars and battles may occur. But you cannot necessarily say that any kind of involvement with war or fighting is evil. God and Buddha consider some wars to be inevitable, so not all of them are evil. Not all historical figures who fought wars and built a country, or served as generals, are devils. Sometimes, such wars are necessary, and there are times when people have to fight hard to protect their citizens.

Moreover, people are at least allowed to fight to protect their families when necessary. If a burglar breaks into a house at night and shoots a few family members living there with a gun or stabs them with a knife to take their valuables, the husband might fight back with violence. He might use a gun if the country allows it. The law of this world considers this self-defense.

A situation like this will call for a trial in this world. The trial may resolve the case, but if that is not enough, it will be taken to the court of Yama for judgment. Situations that are justifiable or require self-defense—situations that will make others think it was inevitable—will be given an allowance.

Suppose Japan, as it is today, is to be involved in a war in the near future. This may not be something I should comment on from my current position, and it should rather be said by the political and military leaders. But imagine that North Korea makes numerous nuclear weapons and one-sidedly shoots them into Japan. Millions or tens of millions of Japanese citizens might die, and North Korea might tell us, "Japan must become a vassal state of North Korea. You must hand over all personal belongings and properties. We will treat you as our slaves from now on."

To prevent this from happening, Japan may develop weapons, fight back, and defend its citizens. But this action of Japan will not be considered evil based on the laws of Yama; it is only a natural response. If North Korea is taking wrongful actions, they are the unforgivable ones, so they will definitely be judged as evil. However, if both sides are wrongful to a certain extent, they will be judged on a case-by-case basis.

Take, for example, the laws of Buddha from 2,500 years ago. Buddha was asked, "In the case of war, are warriors considered guilty of the crime?" He responded, "The primary crime resides with the king." Of course, it is not always the king; nowadays, it could be the prime minister or president, among others. What Buddha meant was, "First, the king will be held responsible for committing sins or not." In other words, the king will be asked, "Was it a righteous war?" If not the king, it could be the generals. They will be judged on whether they did the right thing or not.

The lower you are on the ladder of power, the less accountable you are. For example, a police officer or a military officer is often bound to obey a major order given by his or her superior. If they were ordered to fire volleys at a target, they would certainly follow the order. But they will not necessarily be charged with a crime after death if it was the duty they had to fulfill in the chain of command within the proper legal system. Therefore, not every war or violent action becomes a crime.

However, even an individual can be held accountable if he displays brutality and viciousness that are beyond human nature while fighting a war against an enemy country or another ethnic group. In this case, these individuals will be condemned. For example, in an African country, Hutus and Tutsis killed each other using weapons such as axes and machetes. They probably fought for a reason, but if individuals turn into a mob and start killing people indiscriminately, these killers may be individually held accountable for their sins and be judged in hell.

Those who are judged to be "hellish" during conflicts and wars will go to a place called the Asura Hell or the Asura Realm. There, they will continue to kill each other eternally. For example, during the Battle of Sekigahara (1600) in Japan, the eastern and western armies fought against each other. The person's birthplace determined their side in the war. If you became the winners, you were naturally considered righteous, but some of those who died in that war and have fallen to hell are still unable to get out of there, although their number is decreasing now.

As these spirits continue to kill each other in the Asura Hell, they will come to think, "What a stupid thing I have been doing," and realize their mistakes. Then, they can ascend to heaven, and the number of them in hell will gradually decrease. Sometimes, spirits can reflect on what they have done by watching others who are similar to them.

Materialistic pleasure-seekers arrive at the Hells of the Bloody Pond, Mountain of Needles, and Forest of Razor Leaves

The same is true for the Hell of the Bloody Pond. Those who went far off in their sexual life as a human during their lifetime and have no particular supporting evidence or conditions to be saved will be thrown into a place called the Hell of the Bloody Pond. Like-minded spirits have also gathered there. They will experience this hell until they realize that what they thought was joyful and beautiful and brought them pleasure was actually suffering itself.

A bloody pond is just a symbol; many men and women are drowning in a pond of bloody water. They are floating around naked. Seeing them drowning and floating in this bloody pond will not arouse any earthly sexual desires; all of them look grotesque and monstrous, and it is an unpleasant sight.

The Hell of the Bloody Pond is not enough, so other hells also exist outside of this pond. This is the reality. We are now in the 2020s, but these hells exist even now. The hells described in Buddhism are still a reality; none of them have changed.

The Bloody Pond and the Mountain of Needles are traditional hells. Those who committed evil are chased around by executioners, jailers, or punishers (ogres) in an area where swords are piercing out from the ground. Their body is cut in many ways, and they become bloody all over. This experience is horrible and painful.

The Hell of the Forest of Razor Leaves is also well-known in Buddhism. Here, women seduce men, although they are both in hell. Many of those in this hell used to work in nightlife businesses during their lifetime, and there are also many who were involved with crime.

To describe this hell, a beautiful woman is waiting at a treetop. Underneath the tree is a crowd of spirits filled with lust and sexual desire. "Come over here," she calls out to them, so they all try their best to climb up the tree. But because each leaf on the tree is like a razor blade pointing downward, their bodies will be slashed all over. Then, once they reach the top, the beautiful woman is no longer there; instead, they see her at the bottom of the tree. "Come down. I'm right here," she says again, and when they try to climb down, all the blades are pointing up this time. This kind of hell is called the Hell of the Forest of Razor Leaves.

After all, materialistic pleasure-seekers only see themselves as physical existences, so these hells are trying to teach them in a materialistic way that what they are seeking is not "pleasure." They do not think about what is right or wrong; they can only tell whether something is "pleasure" or "displeasure." Even insects can tell this difference, so this is what these hells are teaching.

At some point in time, they must realize their own mistakes in their materialistic pleasure-seeking attitude. They must realize how foolish such an attitude is. Sexual pleasure can become addictive in the same way as drugs or cocaine. Once people drown in physical pleasures, they will become addicted and can no longer get themselves out. So they have to experience it over and over again until they get sick of it; they will be guided and will come to think, "I want to become a decent person again."

Those who have committed various crimes will be sent to experience multiple hells. There is more than one type of hell, and it is a "mandatory course" for people to go through a number of hells that are related to their greatest evil acts. It seems that an increasing number of people today are going to the hell of sexual desire.

5

Physical Pleasure and the Price to Be Paid in the Afterlife

Self-control distinguishes humans from animals

I want you to at least recognize that human beings are different from animals because this is an important point. You must respect the other person's dignity as a human being, and with this respect, you must love each other as spiritual beings and influence each other to be better. As long as humans have this understanding, they are given a certain allowance to feel some worldly happiness through physical pleasure. But it becomes a problem if you go beyond it and act in a way an animal would act—just as how a male dog unleashed among a number of female dogs would act on them, one after another.

Fox spirits are common in Japan. These spirits often influence the women who use their devil-like or enchantress-like nature to seduce men and corrupt them, tempt them into committing a crime, or make them go down the wrong path. Some women believe that a woman's job is to allure men, but those who are obsessed with increasing their temptress-like sexual charms are spiritually very close to the Hell of Beasts.

In fact, the Hell of the Bloody Pond is located relatively close to the Hell of Beasts, and they are often "convertible" or interchangeable.

Nevertheless, not all animals are like this. For instance, pandas fall in love for only two or three days a year. So zookeepers try hard to get pandas "married" during those two or three days. They even prohibit visitors from watching the pandas and prepare a quiet environment for them in the hope that the pandas will concentrate their spirits and get married. Perhaps pandas, which are aroused for only two days or so a year, are more decent than humans, who are sexually active all year round.

In Japanese *haiku* poetry, there is a seasonal phrase called "a cat's love," which refers to the month of February. When cats become pregnant around February, they give birth around summertime. Summer seems to be the prime time to give birth and raise kittens because there is plenty of food, and they never freeze to death. The season that cats give birth is set around that time. In other months besides February, they are not particularly interested in the opposite sex.

In this way, it might be wrong for you to assume that all animals are lower-level creatures than humans. Note that there are animals that are not aroused all year round, although this may be more of an instinct rather than self-control.

On the contrary, humans can be aroused all year long, and that is why self-control is necessary. You must choose the right time, the right place, and the right partner. You need to ask yourself, "Is it justifiable? Is it appropriate in the eyes of God, Buddha, or my guardian and guiding spirits?"

Buddhism has a teaching of "untimeliness" or "being ill-timed." For example, it is fine for a married couple or people in a serious relationship to be intimate with each other after work when they are relaxed. However, if they are having sex during regular work hours or while their children are still awake, it will have a negative impact. From a Buddhist viewpoint, failing to choose the right time is considered a wrongful act.

The same can be said of choosing the right place. The criminal code considers the display of obscene objects and public lewdness as a crime. In this way, people must not do things in an inappropriate place.

Some may say, "It shouldn't be a problem to strip at a strip club because it's the right place." It sounds like a valid point, but it depends on how the police judge and crack down on them. Apparently, the police do not take a strict stance because a meticulous crackdown can sometimes invite more crimes. So it seems the police sometimes go easy on them; they tighten or loosen their supervision depending on the times. The sex industry itself has many hellish aspects, but if it is completely eliminated, many ordinary women will be assaulted on their way home from work. Thus, the police seem to be "controlling" this situation well. But whether what the police are doing is right or wrong is another question. This is a very difficult point.

Cherish your physical body
as a "holy temple" for the soul to reside

Please do not make a mistake and think, "This physical body is mine. It's at my disposal, so it's up to me to decide how to use it." People say, "I have legs, so what's wrong with kicking a soccer ball and playing soccer?" or "I have arms, so what's wrong with swinging a baseball bat and getting a hit?" On a similar note, many people think, "Humans have the right over their own physical body, so I should be able to use it however I want."

But let me tell you: Your physical body was gifted to you by your parents, so you must be grateful for that. Each of you has been gifted a physical body; your parents gave birth to you and have put a lot of work and energy into raising you. Very few parents raise their children hoping for them to grow into a criminal. Most parents wish for their child to become a successful person who can contribute to the world. They put in every effort so that their children can succeed. Parents do taxing work, cook meals, and sacrifice sleep when their babies cry. Despite these difficulties, they raise their children.

You may enter adulthood and think, "I turned 18" or "I turned 20. I'm free to do whatever I want," but you must be careful of how you use your physical body that was gifted to you by your parents. You must use it so that you can give back to society as well as take responsibility for your future actions. If you live as an irresponsible adult, you may unexpectedly get someone or yourself pregnant and spread misfortune to your children. This is why you need to be aware of your responsibility regarding that.

What is more, it is true that your physical body was given by your parents, but there is a premise to that: "God or Buddha exists. There exists a place called the Spirit World, and there is a system of reincarnation. Humans have been permitted to reincarnate."

Therefore, existentialist thinking is virtually wrong. Some people may have acquired a victim mentality and may think, "I was thrown into this world by chance. You can't choose parents, and I was born into such a terrible family." But the truth is that everyone knows where they will be born before birth. If you chose to be born into a difficult environment, it means you have some kind of challenge to overcome for your spiritual training. Please know this.

I want you to cherish and use your physical body carefully by telling yourself, "My body is a 'holy temple' for my soul to reside." It is neither good nor evil in itself. If you use a knife well, for example, it can be used for cooking or peeling fruit, but it can also turn into a weapon if you use it to kill someone. In the same way, a physical body can become good or evil depending on the mindset of the person using it.

Human rights in this world are not considered in hell

Nowadays, the number of LGBTQ individuals is increasing throughout the world, especially in Western democratic nations. They say they are advocating human rights. As more souls of LGBTQ people are returning to the other world, I have examined what became of them. Unfortunately, as far as I have examined, in hell, there are no such things as "human rights" that people in this world claim.

Earlier I talked about the Hell of the Forest of Razor Leaves. Those who are fitting for such kind of hell may find themselves being chased across many areas where swords grow from the ground. But nowadays, there are also more modernized types of hell. Surgical operation is now common, so tools similar to those used by doctors are being used in hell. For example, in a hospital-type hell, a body is cut with an electric saw or is cut open with a scalpel in surgery.

The fact that this hell exists shows that even some doctors and nurses have forgotten their true mission and lived as evil people. There are evil doctors among those who run hospitals. Not all doctors and nurses are angels, and some of them are in a hospital-type hell and continue to do those things. This makes me feel that times are changing.

In the past, there used to be the Hell of Black Ropes. Black ropes are inked strings that carpenters use to cut a piece of wood for a pillar; on one edge of the wood, he places a piece of the string that has been dipped in dark ink and stretches it to another edge. And when he flicks the string away, a sharp line is drawn across the wood. The carpenter then saws the wood precisely along the line. My grandfather was a shrine carpenter, and I heard he was skilled in using it. His name was Genzaemon, and I heard that people would often say, "There is not a single break in Mr. Gen's inked marking. He can always draw straight, sharp lines."

In the Hell of Black Ropes, this technique is used to cut up human bodies; inked strings are bitterly flicked on top of the spirit's body. Such strings also appear in Jiangshi movies—stories of the Eastern-type zombies that resurrect. These are actually used to cut up human bodies.

This hell existed in the past, but today, there are many hells related to hospitals. Even now, people sometimes visit haunted spots during nighttime, such as abandoned hospitals or hospitals that are no longer operating, to get horror experiences. These hospitals have begun to appear in hell to be used as places for punishment.

So this is what I want to tell you: "You're free to assert your human rights in this world, but if your actions go too far, you will lose your human rights completely in the afterlife. That is why it might be better for you to stop doing it now."

Freedom is important. It is very important, but with freedom comes responsibility. You have to consider, "What will happen to society if everyone follows the freedom I seek?" If society collapses and social order gets disrupted by everyone carrying out what you are doing, then that is not good.

This may be along the lines of what Kant said, but if you think that society will become better after everyone around you copies what you are doing, then that is fine. However, if everyone does something thinking, "I'm the only one who is allowed to do this, and if other people do what I'm doing, it's going to create trouble," then that is a crime and should not be recommended to others. There is a thing called "maxim." You must do things that are acceptable for other people to do the same. Similarly, you should not do anything that is not good for others to imitate.

The use of drugs and stimulants is still strictly regulated and is a crime in Japan, but in many countries, the law is less strict. Oftentimes, drugs and stimulants serve as funding sources for some countries or criminal organizations. Like I said earlier, you might think, "My body is mine, so who cares if I use drugs and stimulants? Whether I live long or die young—it's my choice." That might be one idea, but people are easily influenced, so drug abuse always goes around. Please ask yourself, "What will happen to society if others do the same? What will happen to the next generation and the generation after that?" Then, you will realize that you should stop doing what is undesirable for society.

6

Your Faith, Thoughts, and Actions Will Certainly Be Judged after Death

It is difficult to teach everything about hell; essentially, all things that are related to crime will be judged in hell. In addition, people who have escaped the laws of this world and were not charged guilty or deemed a perpetrator based on civil law can be judged in hell.

That is why "faith" and "what you thought" are important. You should reflect on yourself and mainly examine the Six Worldly Delusions: greed, anger, foolishness, pride, doubt, and false views.

You must also reflect on your "actions." Those who have done many things to harm people's divine nature or Buddha-nature are not easily forgiven. Once you have repented during your lifetime, do the opposite things and make efforts to become a different person.

I could not talk about everything, but this is the reality of hell. Yama's judgment is absolutely real, although its style may differ from country to country. In other words, he might appear as a judge in some places or a high-ranking official in other places; the style of judgment may vary by country, but you will surely be judged.

On another note, there is a religion (Seicho-no-Ie) that claims, "Every child who dies before the age of seven is a high spirit," but that is not true at all. Young children who die before they can think for themselves often end up as lost spirits. They do not know what to do because they have never been taught.

Since ancient times, it has been said in Buddhism, "The souls of departed children stack stones on the Children's Limbo." Indeed, there is a hell where children who died young and have become lost gather together. Guiding angels do visit these children, but they are struggling because the children cannot understand their words. This is the reality. Abortion is common, and in certain cases, it cannot be helped because giving birth may expand the area of hell. But in principle, you must know that a soul resides in a fetus, so if you killed it through abortion or by other means, you should study and understand Buddha's Truth well and offer a prayer of salvation.

There is a group of lawyers that claim, "Memorial service for unborn babies is spiritual fraud," and it could be true if the service is only conducted to make a profit. But the truth is that some children do not know what to do after they die, so they can only rely on their parents. In that case, it is important to hold a memorial service for them. But if the memorial service is conducted by a religious person who does not believe in souls and only holds it to make money, then it should be considered fraud. However, studying the Truth well and providing guidance to those who passed away at a young age is important.

Also, in general, it is human virtue to appropriately pay respect to the dead by making a grave or in other ways. Ever since the economy entered a downturn, these customs have been cut back. More people choose to do as they please, such as scattering the ashes at sea or burying the ashes at the foot of a tree. I do not mean to say that all of these practices are bad, but if they have started from materialistic thinking, people must think twice before doing so. Building graves and conducting funerals are means for humans to culturally pass on the Truth that the other world is real and truly exists. So please value this tradition.

With this, I conclude the chapter.

CHAPTER THREE

Curses, Spells, and Possession

—How to Control Your Mind
So You Do Not Fall to Hell

1

Curses, Spells, and Possession Lead You to Hell

Are you going to heaven or hell?
—It depends on how you live now

I have been giving lectures about hell, and in this chapter, I will narrow it down to specialized themes and talk about curses, spells, and possession. They are associated with religion as a whole as well as with the theme of hell.

I assume most people generally think, "Hell is something to think about after I die" or "I'll just think about what to do if I end up there." However, that is not how things work. You must think about it while you are alive. Whether you will go to heaven or hell is not a question that begins suddenly after you die. You can actually guess where you will go in several years or decades by looking at your life now, including your physical conditions, and especially at your spiritual way of living and your mentality.

The term *hyo-i* (possession) is commonly used in religion, so most of my readers may be familiar with it, but people in general who are not involved with religion might say they have never heard of it or do not know anything about it. Perhaps even people like newscasters or anchorpersons who know about various topics might ask, "What is hyo-i?"

This is slightly off-topic, but the Japanese kanji characters for the word hyo-i (憑依) are difficult. They are difficult to write out and are probably not commonly used.

When I was a first-year student in university, I took a class on political process theory. A professor named Jun'ichi Kyogoku would write the word "憑依 (hyo-i)" on the board and read it as "*hyo-e*." He kept saying *hyo-e* for a whole year. I was going back and forth thinking about whether I should correct him or not, but in the end, I did not tell him. He must have been reading it that way for decades, so I thought he should take responsibility for his mistake. I may have corrected my teacher if I was a middle or high school student.

University classes have a much bigger audience of hundreds of students, but hardly anyone reacted. I guess none of them knew the word and they probably thought that they were learning new vocabulary. The professor read the word incorrectly, and it gave me the impression that he had not studied religion. If you take its literal reading, you could read it the way he did, but *hyo-i* is its correct reading. It means "to possess" or "to haunt," and you will come across this theme in occult-related films and TV shows.

The difference between a curse and a spell

This chapter will cover two concepts: *curse* or *spell* and *possession*. How do they relate to each other?

You can be cursed by or be put under a spell by many people while you are alive. What is the difference between a *curse* and a *spell*? I am not sure of the exact connotation for each word in English, but from my own experience, a "curse" may be caused by trivial matters.

A long time ago, I went to a grocery store to buy a watermelon. I asked the owner, "Is this watermelon ripe?" He shouted at me, saying, "How would I know? Things would be so much easier if I knew that!" I remember feeling offended by being yelled at. This level of verbal abuse would probably be a "curse."

Then, what about a spell? In our previous movie (*Into The Dreams...And Horror Experiences*, original concept by Ryuho Okawa, released in 2021), there is a scene in which a long-black-haired woman in a white kimono nails a straw doll onto a tree in the woods. This would be called a "spell." I get the impression that a spell is a strong wish to send another person to hell in a systematic way.

I am not sure if this is a correct understanding. Even an English language scholar may not know the difference; they probably are not very interested in this kind of topic. After all, it comes down to how people involved in religion use the words; in my case, this is how I understand it.

So if you spit out negative words at another person in a day-to-day quarrel, it would be a "curse."

When I was younger, I visited Greece to do research for my book series about Hermes (four volumes of *Love Blows Like the Wind*). I think I was still in my 30s. In those times, I used to live in Nishi-Ogikubo in the Suginami Ward of Tokyo. When I got back from Greece, I was hungry so I walked into a sushi restaurant in that area. As I was eating sushi, the chef asked me, "You seem tanned. Did you travel somewhere?" So I answered, "I traveled to Greece." He then said, "Ah, a trip to Greece at such a young age. I'm sure it will ruin your later years." What he meant by this is that my later years would not be so great if I were already lavishing money on traveling abroad. Usually, this is not something you would say to a customer, but I suppose it was not what he wanted to hear. I still remember what he said.

This happened more than 30 or maybe 32–33 years ago. You could say it is a bit snobbish for a young man to travel to Greece. I think the chef was older than me, but he was hinting that he did not have the luxury of going to Greece. Frankly, I was working on a book series about Hermes and I needed to go there. That is why I went and traveled around Greece, and I was able to write the story thanks to that.

However, this is what I was told. As a customer who was merely there paying for the food, I was told that my later years would be a mess; it was as if I was cursed. The fact that I am saying this even now might mean that his curse is still haunting me somewhere.

Cursing might involve feelings such as jealousy. Jealousy and envy may not be very deep or serious feelings, but they are negative reactions toward another person that arise as part of basic human emotions. That is why you cannot stop yourself from saying something to them. Once you do, your negative feelings haunt them as if birdlime has stuck onto them. This is what a curse is.

The examples of spells I received from other religious groups

In terms of a spell, you will have thoughts like, "I'll never forgive him. Let's together curse him to death." When your hatred intensifies to this extent, it will become a spell. Earlier, I mentioned the example of a curse—how I was told that my later years would be no good when I talked about my trip to Greece—but spells have also been cast upon me before.

Case 1: A deadly spell cast by a religious group based in Tachikawa City

This happened around the same time as the experience I just mentioned, which was around the year 1990. During those times, I often gave lectures at Yokohama Arena, which has a seating capacity of about 10,000. We started to set up the venue the day before the lecture because we needed to build everything—from the podium to the aisles to the waiting room. We hired a contractor who was familiar with the carpentry work at Yokohama Arena.

Then, I heard the following story from one of my secretaries. My secretaries at the time would tell me everything without considering if it was appropriate or not. So they just told me what they had heard, even though it was right before my lecture. Apparently, the contractor did some work for a religious group based in Tachikawa City a few days before mine. When the religious group heard that I would be next to give a lecture there, those people said, "How dare he! Let's cast a deadly spell." The contractor said that the group was holding a ritual prayer to cast a death spell on me at their dojo.

I wish they had not told me that right before the lecture because it sure did not make me feel great. My secretaries at the time probably thought, "We have to let Master know. We can't let Master die on the podium just like that. We should tell him so he could defend himself."

When I was notified of the situation, I thought, "What? Cast a spell and kill me? Go ahead if they think they can do it." My secretaries did their duty of telling me, and because the group was targeting me, I had no choice but to repel their spell. They were praying, "We shall destroy his lecture!" So I told myself, "I shall repel it!" I do not remember which lecture it was—maybe it was "Love Is Infinite" or another one I gave around then.

After the lecture, I was given more information. The people in that religious group were saying, "Why doesn't he die? Most people die when we cast a spell of this scale on them." I heard this story after my lecture ended safely and successfully. I am not sure if the group was praying with 10-20 people, but they seemed to be wondering, "Why didn't he collapse? Normally, a person passes away, collapses, or is sent to a hospital immediately when we cast this spell with these many members."

This is truly a spell. It is a type of curse that is much more wicked and vicious. It was clear that a devil was involved.

Case 2: A spell cast by an esoteric Buddhist sect in Kyoto

I had an experience of a spell in Kyoto as well. Kyoto Broadcasting System (KBS) has an auditorium-like space, and I once rented the space to hold a seminar for a few hundred people. During my stay in Kyoto, I also became a target of a spell.

The group in Tachikawa City I previously mentioned (Shinnyo-en) is based on esoteric Buddhism, and there is another group of the same kind in Kyoto. Its founder has already passed away, but it gained popularity in the 1970s, about 10 years before Happy Science was founded. The founder was older than me. He had been leading his group for a long time, but it could not gain popularity for a while. I think his wife was a dentist, and he was living off of her income to operate his group for several decades.

But one day, his books such as *Esoteric Buddhist Astrology* suddenly became a bestseller. He advocated things like, "Esoteric Buddhism can change your fortune" and "If you have bad parents, cut off the karma between parent and child." Just like the discipline of 1,000-Day Circumambulation, he upheld a "1,000-Day Seating Meditation Discipline" and said, "If you meditate in a particular sitting posture for 1,000 days, you'll be able to cut off bad spiritual ties between parent and child and improve your fortune."

He also popularized certain expressions like, "Turn your channel." He simplified the teaching and said, "Just turn your channel; then, your wavelengths can tune to a different place, and your life will change." This is much like the idea that you can instantly attain Buddhahood in your lifetime. He taught, "You just need to change the channel of your mind; then, you can instantly become superhuman." His group then gained popularity and became a sensation to some extent. Some of their members worked for an advertising agency, so the group had help from professionals.

People of this religious group seemed to bear a grudge against me, and they tried to put a deadly spell on me. Upon hearing the news of my coming to Kyoto, they cast a spell on me, but my seminar ended without any problem. I do not know why, but I somehow learned later that the founder was exclaiming, "Why isn't he dead!? Anyone I put a spell on should die." (The group's name is Agon Shu, a Buddhist sect based on Agama Sutras, otherwise known as Kiriyama Esoteric Buddhism.)

Evil esoteric Buddhist sects are often like this. They are similar to voodoo; the practitioners have the ability to cast death spells. They can do this probably because they believe their target is a devil.

Nevertheless, I heard later that his spell was repelled and he collapsed as he was doing some kind of ritual.

Your mind will be tuned to hell
if it constantly emits negative vibrations

If the target person is, in fact, evil and is trying to make the world a bad place, a curse or a spell can actually knock that person down. In that case, the spell will not be repelled and will have an effect. But if the target person is making diligent and serious efforts in their spiritual discipline, then the spell can be repelled. This is called the "method of the mirror"— the fundamental countermeasure against a spell.

The longer people live, they will often invite various people's hate and jealousy to themselves or will unintentionally hurt other people with their words. To not blindly walk into trouble at such times, it is important to always be ready to repel curses and spells for self-protection.

If you respond to anger with anger, and if both sides keep on retaliating, the situation will only get worse. This often happens in domestic violence or quarrels; when you verbally abuse your partner, the partner will argue back. Then, the situation will escalate, and the more you argue, the more he or she argues back. Soon, a physical fight breaks out. It will start with your fists and legs, and once you start punching and kicking, one might bring out a kitchen knife and the other might fight back by throwing pots and pans. This is a story I have actually heard of. Such things do gradually escalate.

So it is very important to not take others' negative words to your heart. When you hold grudges against someone, curse them, or become furious toward them, it can cause disharmony not only in your own mind but also in the other person. If your mind is disturbed in this way and this state continues, in other words, your mind is always emitting negative vibrations, the mind will gradually tune to a realm in hell where spirits with similar vibrations as yours gather.

Some spirits cannot even go to hell but are still wandering around this world, looking for other people with a similar mindset. Based on the Law of Same Wavelengths, when a living person emits similar thoughts to those of the spirits in hell, or of evil spirits or malicious spirits wandering on earth, the spirits are drawn to the person as if drawn to a magnet.

If it is only a temporary feeling that soon subsides, then these spirits cannot possess you for long. It is like the surface of a lake. When you throw a stone into a lake, ripples are formed at first, but after a while, it will calm down and the ripples will disappear. In the same way, you become capable of repelling those spirits. But if you keep throwing stones into a lake one after another, the water will always be disturbed; likewise, your mind can constantly be in an agitated state.

As you keep emitting bad, rough-waves-like vibrations for a certain period of time, you will be in tune with like-minded spirits, even if you do not know what kinds of vibrations you are emitting in a religious sense. To use the phrase mentioned earlier—"turn your channel"—your "channel" will be tuned to like-minded spirits, and they will come to you.

2

The Three Poisons of the Mind That Are Tuned to Hell: Greed, Anger, and Foolishness

Greed: Japanese folktales warn of excessive desire

I have been speaking about negative thoughts. As I often say in my teachings, the most typical ones are the Three Poisons of the Mind—greed, anger, and foolishness.

Greed means to have excessive desire. It is exemplified by the greedy old couple in Japanese folktales. The folktales often depict the retribution a greedy person has to face.

Take, for example, the story of *The Old Man Who Made Flowers Bloom*. An old couple has a dog that keeps barking in their backyard, so the old man digs the spot where the dog is barking and finds many treasures. Upon hearing that, a greedy old couple who lives next door asks him to lend the dog. The greedy old man forcibly takes the dog and urges it to bark. Reluctantly, the dog starts barking. But when he digs the spot, he does not find any treasure; instead, various junk and monstrous creatures come out. The greedy old man gets outraged and kills the dog he borrowed.

The owners of the dog bury their beloved dog and make a grave for it. Then, a tree grows there, and when they cut it down, burn it, and scatter the ashes around withered cherry blossom trees, a miracle occurs: flowers bloom one after another. Hearing this, a local lord comes passing by and rewards the old man who made the flowers bloom. The greedy old man says, "I, too, can easily make flowers bloom," and he tries to do the same; but the flowers do not bloom, and the greedy man gets punished.

This story tells us that since olden times, people have believed that those with excessive desire will suffer punishment in some way or another in this world. Or rather they believed that some kind of divine punishment must befall them according to the law of cause and effect.

So being greedy is a vice. Excessive greed has been considered a vice that gives birth to various evils.

This is generally true. There is nothing wrong if people are living in a way that is appropriate to their level, but some people crave more than what they deserve.

I just mentioned the story about the miracle that an old couple next door experienced, but the same can be said about the lottery. Simply hearing the news that your next-door neighbor won the first prize in a lottery may well disturb your mind. A part of you might think, "Why can't I win?" And you may be tempted to take out your irritation on someone or something. Greed comes out in various forms in this way.

Greed and the urge to do evil as seen among former and prospective students of prestigious schools

Some people may flare up with jealousy just by seeing other people getting good grades from studying. For example, the prestigious Kaisei High School conducts a famous sports event every year, and I once spotted an article in a newspaper that said a fire broke out during this event. It happened in the storage room that contained physical education equipment, and a fire truck was called. It was found out that the offender was a graduate of Kaisei High School. He had been promised that once he entered Kaisei, he would have a successful future, but things did not turn out the way he expected. So he felt the urge to start a fire and cause a commotion as he walked past the students who were enjoying the sports event. I remember reading that long ago.

There is another story. In the past, college-preparatory schools were popular, although I am not sure if this still holds true today. Nowadays, there are fewer children, so the situation may be different from the past. But in the old days, there were not enough colleges and universities to accommodate everyone who wanted to attend, and the construction of new schools was not enough to solve the issue. So about half of the applicants had to study an extra year to pass an entrance exam the following year. This situation lasted for quite a while.

Among college-preparatory schools, Sundai Preparatory School was especially known for sending many students to the most competitive universities in Japan. The top-performing students at this prep school were enrolled in the "morning course." The morning course had classes for both humanities and sciences, and about half of the students who attended this course got accepted into the University of Tokyo.

There was a student who said that he felt the urge to throw a bomb into that building. He was saying that if the building was blown up, 200–300 students, who would otherwise go to the University of Tokyo, would die, and this would create more seats and less competition to get into the university. This, too, is a problem that concerns greed. Or perhaps it is not only about greed but also about the overlapping anger and foolishness, which I will cover next.

Anger: What to do when you are raging with anger from not being able to win

Next is anger or losing your temper. People, in general, do get angry; it is also the same for animals. Animals will fight back against any enemies that target and attack them.

A fight between a dog and a cat is quite a scene. When the dog barks, the cat arches its back, bristles its fur and tail, and hisses. The cat knows it is physically inferior to the dog, so it waits for the right moment to land a fatal blow; it becomes tense and gets ready to scratch the dog's nose when the dog attacks. The dog also knows this, so it cannot make a move until the cat is off guard. It is much like a tense kendo match. Sometimes, one of them might suddenly run away if it feels it is no match for the other.

This also happens in the human realm. Where there is competition, there arises disparity between the superior and the inferior. Some people will come to harbor thoughts such as, "I want to ruin others," "I want to be the only winner," or "I want to drive him out of his position." Anger is something that naturally arises, and it will not cease unless you know the religious Truth.

Take, for example, an audition for a female role. Many beautiful women come to audition, so some may get frustrated and think, "There's no way I can get the role with this many people." Even a famous actress who won an Academy Award said, "In an audition, you'll see a hundred other people who are just as pretty as you. I went for a hundred of these and failed a hundred times."

Apparently, the actress who played the role of Gwen in *The Amazing Spider-Man* (Emma Stone) experienced this. Even someone like her, who won the Academy Award, said she auditioned a hundred times and got rejected all one hundred times when she was first starting out. This means that there are already many equally charming or good-looking girls in the world, and it is easy to gather a hundred of them. So it must be quite tough.

At such times, it is important to maintain peace in your mind and keep polishing and training yourself instead of just being envious, resentful, or angry toward others. But this is not an easy thing to do.

The world does not revolve around you, and not everything will go right for you and only you. Others are also striving for their own self-realization, success, and happiness. It is hard to know what "prize" will be appropriate for you, like in a lottery; you will not know what is right or appropriate for you unless you go through life.

There are times when your efforts do not bear fruit. You will certainly come across such a period, but you need to tell yourself that you are being tested during that time. When your efforts do not bear fruit, you are being tested to see if you will give up or not.

The competitive ratio can be one in tens, one in hundreds, or even one in thousands, so the more people give up, the less competition there will be. This is also a blessing because people will not have to compete to death.

Some people would eventually give up during trials and adversity, whereas others are waiting for the number of competitors to decrease. But if you continue making efforts regardless of what happens, at some point in time, you may be given the best opportunity to attain the results you want. When such a time comes, you are tested to see if you can grasp the opportunity.

Life is tough, but holding grudges or resentment toward other people will not make it much better. Please continue to keep doing what you can do and wait for an opportunity to come your way.

If opportunity does not arise, another path will open up

However, there are times when opportunities do not come to you. In that case, it is the Divine Will, so there is nothing you can do about it. The Divine Will may be telling you, "Find a new profession" or "There is another path for you." Some people may audition for a role and win it by chance, only to get a bad reputation after one film and fade out from the movie industry. You never know what will bring happiness.

Here is something I heard from the owner of a watch shop that I go to. After he graduated from Waseda University, Faculty of Law, he was studying for the bar exam while taking on a part-time job at a department store, where he would bring watches to the customers and sell them. As he had continued to study for the exam for several years, he was at a mature age compared with the other students who worked part-time. This earned him more credibility and sales than the others who worked there. Because he brought in higher sales, he continued working there until it became his main profession. Eventually, he opened his own watch shop and has been working there for several decades now.

He was studying for the bar exam but was running a watch shop before he realized it. This change of course in life is something that he, himself, would not have imagined. Even he did not probably know he could sell more watches than the other part-time clerks at the department store.

For the bar exam, he read books and worked hard to memorize judicial precedents and the law. He continued to take the exam year after year; meanwhile, he worked selling watches. He said he went all the way to Tokushima Prefecture and sold watches at the Marushin Department Store there. He had been selling watches for several years, so he was older than the other part-timers; customers felt that he had more life experience and credibility. They probably saw him as the senior sales associate of the watch store.

Unexpectedly, he demonstrated his talents in this watch business and acquired a lot of knowledge. As he went through manuals of various brands of watches and sold them, he naturally learned about watches and memorized the details. He began to import watches himself and sell them until, eventually, he opened his own shop.

Such a life is possible, so it is best not to drive yourself into the corner and limit yourself by thinking, "This is all I have."

The kind of person who can run a watch shop and be successful is not really suited to become a judge or a prosecutor. Some lawyers may become successful if they are scheming with words, but lawyers are not salespeople. Ever since the 19th century, there has been a Japanese term *sanbyaku-daigen* (lit. a shyster who would take on a case for very cheap money—300 coins—and uses trickery to win the case). Just like that, some lawyers might practice law as a mere business and work only to win cases, even by lying or deceiving. In the Japanese TV drama *Legal High*, Lawyer Komikado wins all the cases he takes on, but lawyers who have a strong salesperson-like mentality might lose their credibility. They need to keep calm and be collected to some extent.

It is hard to know what kind of talent you have. But if you live sincerely, a path will open up for you at some point. When I was young, I read the phrase: "In life, when one door closes, another door opens," and I really believe this is true.

Looking back at my own life, I, too, have studied many things and done various kinds of work. From an overall perspective, my main role now is a religious leader. And what serves as the backbone of my extensive work is the fact that I know various types of people, including foreigners; I have met them and spoken to them, and I have visited various places and studied various kinds of topics.

If someone were to hold a lecture on curses, spells, and possession as the main part of their work, then naturally not many people would come. People who are fond of religion might, but ordinary people would not attend a lecture like that. Even if the person talked about it at university, only the students majoring in religion—so, only a couple of students—might attend. This is how things are.

Foolishness: Not knowing Buddha's Truth invites ignorance

Following greed and anger, the next element is foolishness or ignorance. It originally means "not knowing Buddha's

Truth." There are numerous people who do not know Buddha's Truth in this world. Those who have high societal status, social credibility, and good educational background or who are highly knowledgeable can be completely ignorant of the religious truth. It is a shame.

For example, doctors generally do the work of bodhisattva by saving people's lives; likewise, nurses are called "angels in white." If they do good work with good intentions, they can return to a world of angels or bodhisattvas. But there are various types of doctors and nurses, including those who treat their patients poorly or make medical mistakes over and over again. They may suffer from a guilty conscience or, on the contrary, take actions that are borderline illegal.

So your profession is not the only factor that determines your destination. Whatever your profession may be, the essential points are "the kind of thoughts you had while living" and "the kind of achievements you have left behind."

Ignorance of religious truth is prevalent in the field of medical science, and it has even spread to the field of religious studies and Buddhist studies. Some professors give lectures on Buddha's teachings and Buddhism while believing, "There's no such thing as a spirit or soul" or "God or Buddha does not exist." Some of them think, "Buddha may have existed in the past, but now he's just a carved, wooden Buddha statue." Others think, "The bronze statue of the seated Buddha is hollow inside. Be it the one in Kamakura or Nara, it is empty inside and tourists can look inside it. It is empty, so it's obvious the soul is not there. What's the use of praying to those statues that tourists and students on field trips can visit, go inside of, and climb up the stairs to take a look at?"

So there are people who believe that the Buddha statue made out of bronze, wood, or marquetry is actually Buddha. They are at such a level of awareness and only have a cultural understanding of it. Some researchers even believe, "Buddha was a primitive man of the Jomon period (around 14,500 BC to 300 BC), so there's no way he could give high-level teachings. If we interpret them in the modern context, they are no big deal."

a) Ignorance of translating Confucian teachings superficially by removing the dignified tone

The same can be said with the study of Confucianism. I will not comment on whether Confucius was a great man, but *The Analects* can hold a certain powerful tone if they are translated in a noble, dignified way. However, if they are translated into a simple modern language that is easy to understand, many parts may contain no significance.

For example, there is a saying in *The Analects*, "And is it not delightful to have men of the kindred spirit come to one from afar?" What if this line was translated into something like, "My friends came from far away. It would be fun to be together"? I cannot help but feel that it sounds too shallow or unintelligent. If you read, "Some friends, who are far away and whom I can't see often, came to visit me. It's going to be fun," you would question why you should be grateful to learn such a thing.

To take another example, Confucius was asked, "Is there a world after death?" He responded, "If we don't know life, how can we know death?" These words mean, "Before you even come to know about life in this world and its meaning, how would you know about the afterlife?" When this is said in a dignified and noble manner and if you imagine its meaning by feeling its divine tone, it becomes an important teaching.

This phrase teaches the people who are living: "First, correct your current life before thinking about life after death. You must first live your life in the right way now. Only then should you consider the afterlife." If you take his words with good intention, they can be understood like this: "No matter how much you think about the world beyond death, if you are no good in the present, there's no way you can be good in the afterlife. There's no point in fretting over it. So do your best in the present. Live the best possible life now. The outcome in the afterlife will follow."

b) The mistake in the interpretation by the Tendai School and the True Pure Land School of Buddhism

Some people might ask, "I've done all kinds of bad things, but will you do something for me so I can go to heaven after I die?" These people may go to esoteric Buddhism and seek "instant" salvation, just like how cup noodles can be made in three minutes.

I do not want to criticize them too much, and perhaps the practitioners of the Tendai School of Buddhism on Mt. Hiei have some grudge against me. But they only take a part of Buddha's teachings and say, "Human beings have Buddha-nature. We are all children of Buddha, so everyone is already a buddha."

Practitioners of various Buddhist schools climbed Mt. Hiei to undergo Buddhist training, but they all wondered: "Why do we need to train ourselves if we are originally enlightened and are children of Buddha with Buddha-nature?" They were unable to answer this question. Even after they completed a few years of Buddhist training on Mt. Hiei—sometimes 10–20 years—many of those practitioners climbed down without finding the answer.

This is true even now. Some Buddhist practitioners said they finally found the answer after encountering Happy Science and reading my books. I think it was in the 1990s; two Buddhist priests, "Dai-sojo" monks (the highest level in Buddhist priesthood), of the Tendai School, became our regular members, now called "devotee members," at the same time. One of them had completed the "1,000-Day Circumambulation" training. I think there were only three or so people in Japan who completed this training after World War II; the training consists of walking tens of miles for 1,000 days. This person said, "Actually, I wasn't sure if I would really be able to become a buddha by completing the practice of circumambulation. But after I read Happy Science books, I understood for the first time that enlightenment is something different. That's why I joined Happy Science."

From the perspective of different religious groups, I sometimes speak out on things that may sound hostile to them. But even among their believers, some are pure-heartedly seeking faith and can understand and accept what I teach.

A problem lies in the teachings of the True Pure Land Buddhism as well; it teaches that no matter how bad a person may be, Amitabha Buddha will save them. But depending on how it is used, it can either help or bring harm to people.

Some people might say, "I've done too many bad things throughout my life. Is there no chance for me to be saved?" If the practitioners of the True Pure Land Buddhism use its teaching in a good way, they can tell them, "Even if you lived a bad life, you still have a chance as long as you are alive. Change your mind, practice the teachings, and contribute to the world; then, there is still a path to enlightenment for you."

But they could also misuse it and say, "Of course, you can be saved because the sutra says that even an evil person can be saved." Some of them say, "You will be saved if you chant Amitabha Buddha's name 10 times" or "If you chant Amitabha Buddha's name just once, Amitabha will save you." Others even go as far as to say, "The moment you make up your mind and think about chanting the name of Amitabha Buddha, you are already saved." At this point, however, their teaching is like super-instant cup noodles.

Cup noodles can be cooked in three minutes after pouring boiling water into them and closing the lid. Wait three minutes, and it will be ready. To use the metaphor of cup noodles, the True Pure Land Buddhism is making the teaching simpler and simpler, as if to say, "No, you don't need to wait three minutes. It will be ready in just a minute. Actually, the noodles are as good as cooked the moment you think about pouring boiling water. It's already set in stone that way. By the time you think of pouring boiling water, or even as you fill water into a pot and turn on the stove, the noodles are already cooked." I can understand that they would develop the teaching in such a way, but at this level, they have gone too far.

To put this in terms of a criminal offense, suppose a person stabs another with a knife and is sentenced to 10 years in prison. The above teaching is similar to telling this person who is about to go to jail and pay for his crime: "The fact that you are going to jail for 10 years means that you have already been released. You will be out of jail in 10 years anyway, so entering jail is the same as already being released." Certainly, the person will eventually be released, as he was not sentenced to death, but we must question such a way of thinking.

In reality, many of those who are sentenced to 10 years of imprisonment are not kept in prison for the full 10 years. In the majority of cases, their prison term is slightly reduced based on their attitude of remorse, attitude toward work, change in personality, and whether they read books or became more polite. All these aspects are observed and taken into consideration. After all, a *process* lies between the cause and effect, and some kind of *condition* is added between the cause and effect.

Suppose someone was sentenced to 10 years of imprisonment. He may have repented what he did—perhaps he read a book written by Shinran[2] and made an effort to smile at others and say loving words—and now he is released in 8 years instead of 10. If he feels, "Oh, I owe this all to Amitabha Buddha. I'm deeply grateful," he has very much rehabilitated.

On the contrary, he may not repent and show a defiant attitude after receiving a 10-year sentence. He might say,

"Well, I killed that man because he was a bad guy. He had it coming. I just killed him on behalf of heaven. The evil man was roaming around because the police were too slow to do something about it. That guy would've committed more evil deeds and crimes, so I prevented that by killing him. I did a good deed. I gave him the punishment of heaven or rather a 'punishment of a man.'" Even if he is released from prison after serving his 10-year term, someone like this will most likely come back to jail after several months because he has not changed.

Scholars who are ignorant of the Truth will go to hell even if they are not evil in a worldly sense

To misunderstand the good and bad of your thoughts and actions in a religious sense will lead to serious consequences. Some people still go to hell even if they do not meet the criteria of an "evil person" in this world. Some scholars had nothing to do with crime in this world, and they never violated civil law; they have never been sued for a wrongful act or punitive damage. As a scholar, they just conducted research, wrote books, and held classes or lectures every now and then. They were quite serious and diligent in their research, but even so, they fell to hell. This is because what they thought of as the "Truth" was absolutely wrong. To write a book about the wrong ideas and spread them to others counteracts the ordinary, rightful missionary work of religion.

There was a scholar who meticulously studied Buddhism, deeply delved into ancient sutras, and restored them by translating Sanskrit into modern language. But the conclusion he arrived at was this: "Shakyamuni Buddha taught that there is neither a spirit nor a soul. Buddha's idea of *anatman*, or egolessness, teaches that spirits and souls do not exist. Religions in India before Buddha's time had the idea of *atman*; they taught that human beings have a soul, and the soul leaves the body when they die. However, Buddha emerged as a revolutionary philosopher; he flipped this idea around and taught that spirits and souls do not exist."

The scholar then thought: "Spirits and souls don't exist, so our life ends when we die. That's why all things are impermanent, and all phenomena are egoless. We simply return to the soil after we die. And nirvana means that when we die, our soul disappears, just like how the flame of a candle is blown out. This is the explanation of 'the impermanence of all things,' 'the egolessness of all phenomena,' and 'the perfect tranquility of nirvana.' This is the truth."

However, this is not the kind of conclusion one should reach from their research; this is something ordinary people would think if they had never been taught anything. At the very least, most people who only study school textbooks that are approved by Japan's Ministry of Education today will think, "Once a human dies, that's the end." People normally do not know any better because that is all that is written in textbooks.

Some school textbooks write about how people of the ancient Jomon or Yayoi (ca. 300 BC to ca. 250 AD) period believed in life after death. Back then, people buried the dead in an earthen jar, or they broke the legs of the dead, put them in a shape of a fetus, and placed a heavy stone on the stomach before burying them. That was because people were worried that the dead would come back to life. Some accounts about the ancient era say that ancient people believed in the soul and the spirit. But apart from that, we do not learn that there are souls in reality, either in social studies or in science classes.

Ghosts and devils appear in horror movies as a form of entertainment, but as of today, their existence is not academically accepted as scientific truth. This is a shame, but it is the reality.

In the United States, at the end of President Trump's presidency and even during President Biden's term, the government announced that there were cases of unidentified aerial phenomena, although they were not sure of what they were. During Mr. Trump's term, they presented three cases detected by NASA, or rather the Air Force, that were thought to be extraterrestrial and not Earth-originated. During Mr. Biden's presidency, they presented about 140 cases. They could not identify what the phenomena were and used terms such as unidentified flying objects (UFOs). Nevertheless, they acknowledged that there are UFOs. Many other countries also have had similar incidents.

When it comes to the Japanese government, the official response remains the same: "We have not received a single case of a UFO sighting." They do not admit even a single UFO case. In Japan, UFOs are discussed on gossip TV shows or special TV programs featuring paranormal or horror phenomena. UFO manias also post or share pictures of what seems to be UFOs, but the official response by the government is that there is not a single sighting. Even if a pilot of Japan Air Self-Defense Force or commercial airplanes such as JAL or ANA witnesses a UFO, it is not officially reported to the government out of fear that the pilot would be deemed mentally insane. There are countless cases like these, and they demonstrate "ignorance of the Truth."

3

Pride, Doubt, and False Views Lead to Curses, Spells, and Possession

Problems of having pride and doubt

In addition to the Three Poisons of the Mind, there are pride, doubt, and false views.

Too much pride will make you conceited like a *tengu* (a long-nosed goblin). This is also a mindset that will lead you to your downfall. Some people might say, "I stand above everyone," "I was born great," or "I'm distinguished because I've met this-and-that condition." But if you think of yourself as exceptional, special, and a god-like person, you are apt to make mistakes.

Next is doubt. In the current world, doubt is spread by science combined with the mass media. Some people say, "You must doubt, doubt, and doubt everything until you are sure that it's undoubtable. Only then can you say it's true and authentic." Sometimes, this can be right, but in the process of doubting, you might end up seeing everything as a lie, a deception, or a fraud. This is the problem.

Certainly, Shakyamuni Buddha once said something like, "I'm pursuing the kind of Truth that cannot be doubted no matter how hard I try." Those who resonate with such a statement might get caught up in this idea and overlook his other teachings. But if you read Buddha's teachings as a whole, you will find an endless number of mystical phenomena in them. Wanting to disregard the entirety of such phenomena and seeing what is left after doubting and denying everything is also doubt—one of the worldly delusions.

a) The mistake of doubting and denying Buddha's teachings and his biography from the perspective of modern medical knowledge

Some people take a portion of his teachings and deny it by saying, "Buddha is an ancient man, after all. He didn't know things." For example, Shakyamuni Buddha once said in his sermon, "How is it that a baby is born in a proper form when food is digested in the stomach and is excreted?" Back in Buddha's times, the stomach and the uterus were not distinguished on the surgical plane. But some medical experts might only take this part and say, "Oh, with his level of medical knowledge, none of his teachings are worth reading." I am sure there are people like that. However, it is wrong to merely pick out a particular phrase and deny the rest out of skepticism.

At another time, Shakyamuni Buddha said, "Human beings get old and wrinkly; their hair turns gray, and they become hairless; their back bends, and they become feeble. They become as old as a wrecked cart that is held together with a leather strap, and eventually, they die." Buddha left such teaching in his later years. But some cosmetic surgeons might say, "No, that's not necessarily true. There is cosmetic surgery nowadays, and you can keep your youthful appearance forever."

Perhaps cosmetic surgery can make people appear younger, but even so, it cannot grant them eternal life. Even if there is a woman who looks physically young and makes others say, "Wow! Is she really 80 years old? Who would've guessed?" she will still get sick and die. So we cannot say that the teachings are all wrong just because some of them sound unrealistic.

What is more, Shakyamuni Buddha's biography describes that immediately after birth, he stood up and walked toward each of the four directions: north, east, south, and west. Animals can stand on the day they were born. A baby deer or a baby horse can stand up immediately after birth because otherwise, it would be attacked by wild predators. But a human being cannot walk right away.

According to the biography, however, Buddha was able to walk seven steps and said, "In heaven and earth, I alone am to be revered," as he walked in each of the four directions. On reading it, those studying medical science might be skeptical and say, "That's not possible. I do hear about miracles like an illness or cancer being cured once in a while, but it is just impossible for a baby to walk seven steps immediately after birth. Based on this, I guess everything is all nonsense." However, it is wrong to doubt everything because of that one description.

This story is meant to teach people: "Buddha was born as a baby, but in his body resided a noble soul of an adult, or even beyond an adult. You must understand it that way." Earlier, I said that no one is born great, but the opposite is also true, and some people are actually born great. You must understand this holiness. Buddha may have had a father, a mother, an uncle, siblings, or an older servant, but the one who is born as Buddha is sacred since birth. Please do not forget that. The story contains this teaching.

b) The mistake of doubting and denying all mystical phenomena in Buddhist scriptures from the perspective of biology

Another instance is when Shakyamuni Buddha converted three fire-worshipers, the Kasyapa brothers. The eldest of the brothers, Uruvilva Kasyapa, had about 500 disciples. The second brother had about 300, and the youngest brother had about 200 disciples.

Buddha visited the three fire-worshiper brothers to convert them, and at that time, the three brothers made Buddha stay in a cave to test him. When Buddha asked for a place to stay overnight, they told him, "We don't have a room, but there is a cave. Please spend the night there."

In this cave was a poisonous snake. The three brothers had been testing other practitioners who came over to them; in most cases, the visitors who stayed overnight in that cave were bitten by the poisonous snake and died. Because the practitioners would lose their lives there, the three brothers thought it was a good opportunity to kill Buddha as well.

The Buddhist scriptures tend to exaggerate stories, so this may not be true, but the poisonous snake was actually a fire dragon that breathed fire. It would be awful if there was a fire-breathing dragon inside the cave. Whether they really existed or not, I will not go into the details, but maybe it was more like a lizard or a snake, as it sometimes sticks out a tongue as red as a flame. The dragon could have just been a metaphor; nevertheless, it was most probably a poisonous snake—perhaps a giant cobra of some sort.

The Kasyapa brothers had Shakyamuni Buddha stay there overnight, and when they went to the cave the next morning, they were shocked to see Buddha still alive. "What's going on? Why is he still alive?" they exclaimed. To their surprise, the poisonous snake had become very small, and Buddha came out with a small snake sitting on something like a tray. In this way, the Buddhist scripture describes how the giant snake became very small.

This is a miraculous incident. This story is written in Buddhist scripture as one of the mystical phenomena.

If biology teachers read this story only, they would say, "That's impossible. A fire-breathing snake on Earth would be a dragon. Although it's possible for dragon-like creatures to have existed, could they have breathed fire? Today's Godzilla breathes radioactive fire, but suppose a dragon existed 2,500 years ago; would it have breathed fire?" They would have these kinds of doubts.

Nevertheless, various legends talk of creatures that breathe fire. We cannot physically see the creatures to research them, so I wonder if they are real. But legends from the United Kingdom also talk about dragons that breathed fire. Were they real? Were they living creatures or artificial beings? They could have been artificially made in outer space, or they could have been extraterrestrial animals. It could be any of these. Even if there was indeed a creature like this, people might say, "There's no way it can shrink and become smaller. How can its body become so small?

A body can't become small as if shrunk with *Doraemon*'s shrink ray. It's impossible."

So what is this story trying to tell us?

There is another instance where Shakyamuni Buddha tamed a drunken elephant. The story goes that Devadatta set Buddha up by unleashing a drunken elephant that went wild and violent; it trampled several people to death. The elephant stood in front of Buddha and lifted its forelegs, but suddenly it was tamed. It bowed like a puppy, became quiet, and laid down in a way that elephants would do for people to get atop. Such a story is handed down.

This may well be a true story. I say this because even today, some people can use the power of *chi* to tame animals, including wild ones, and even make them fall asleep. I assume that Buddha had the power to control the minds of animals to a certain extent.

In light of this, the story of the poisonous snake could also be true. It is not certain if the snake actually shrank in size, but it is possible that the poisonous snake was tamed and lost its hostility. Cobras, for example, spread out their bodies very wide to make themselves look bigger. They intimidate others by making themselves look taller and larger, but they may look small once they let go of any hostility and calm down, curling up tight. So it is better to not deny everything based on doubt alone.

False views: Ideas that have deviated from the Truth will lead to curses, spells, possession, and hell

After greed, anger, foolishness, pride, and doubt come "false views." It is said that "false views" contain 62 views, but there actually seems to be no end to these views because there are many different kinds of mistaken ideas.

For example, there are six major newspapers in Japan, and they all have different editorials and perspectives. It is hard to tell which ones are right and which ones are wrong, but I am sure that many of their opinions have deviated from the Truth. You must discard the wrong opinions one by one and strive to get closer to the Truth.

Those who have wrong ideas and conduct wrong actions tend to receive curses or put curses on other people while alive. As they constantly think and do the wrong things and receive evil spiritual influence from other people, they can have these negativities "stick" onto their bodies. When this happens, they can be possessed by an evil spirit from hell or an evil spirit wandering on earth that is of a similar mindset.

They may continue to be possessed if the spirit is not removed. If they are possessed by just one spirit, we cannot be sure if they will fall to hell, but if they are possessed by four, five, or six spirits, it is almost certain. Even if they defend themselves in front of Yama, it is obvious that they triggered and caused the possession. People must know this.

Life will get easier by getting rid of these possessions. Your body will feel lighter, and at times, a new path will open up in your life. So thoroughly check whether the cause of possession lies within you.

Even if there is no cause in your mind, you may happen to have had a connection to a certain place. Nowadays, things like stigmatized property are popular in TV shows and movies. Some residences are cheap because suicides have consecutively occurred there or someone was killed. There are movies that feature people who rent these places for fun. But the place could be truly contaminated with evil, so you should not happily seek to have a connection to such places. The mind that seeks these connections can be one of the reasons your outcomes are bad.

You cannot live a good life if you deliberately and happily rent a stigmatized property where spirits curse and cast bad spells. Realtors who knowingly introduce such property to those people are also creating misfortune, so they will not be able to live a good life either. Please avoid situations where you could be possessed in this way.

As a result of curses and spells, or of living a kind of life that invites them, people will most likely experience a phenomenon called possession while they have a physical body. Oftentimes, they will be diagnosed by a psychiatrist as having a mental illness because they engage in a lot of odd behavior or lose chunks of memory of when they are doing something.

For example, there are people who assaulted others and stabbed them with a knife but do not remember doing it. Their personality must have switched at that time. That happens because their soul was away from the body while another spirit entered and took over it. In such cases, their criminal responsibility will certainly be examined, but they will not be asked whether they were possessed. However, the issue of criminal responsibility is closely related to possession.

4

How to Prevent Yourself from Falling to Hell

You will know which hell you will go to by simply reflecting on your life

I can understand why some people worry about whether they would go to heaven or hell. But as the earlier quote of Confucius says—"If we don't know life, how can we know death?"—you do not need to ask a psychic or a spiritual expert to know where you will go after death. You will know it just by examining the life you are living.

What kind of thoughts do you have? If you are living the kind of life that would burn others to death with your flames of jealousy, you will go to the Hell of Scorching Heat. If you are involved with violence and bloodshed, you will most likely go to a place called the Asura Hell or the Hell of Villains. If you are living a corrupt life driven by lust, in most cases, you will be dragged over to the Hell of the Bloody Pond or somewhere near there.

Apart from these, as I have been saying, there are ideological criminals who have mistaken ideologies, be it religious philosophy or political philosophy. Some people advocate the wrong philosophies and make many people unhappy. Those with wrong political thoughts—especially found among leftists—those with wrong religious thoughts, and those who have influenced many people with wrong fundamental ideas and led them astray will all go to a deep, deep place called the Abysmal Hell. It is like the pit of a well, and they cannot get out of it. This is where they will fall into.

So there is no need to ask, "Which hell will I go to?" Reflect on your life, and you shall know it. Please think about it deeply.

Make an effort to turn your mind into a mirror and wipe off bad thoughts

With the help of this chapter, please think once more about curses, spells, and possession in your everyday life.

Diseases such as rheumatism may have a worldly cause, but viewed spiritually, people with rheumatism are, in many cases, possessed by various spirits such as snake spirits. The same can be said about shoulder problems, including stiff or frozen shoulders, and about ailments such as not being able to stand up because of a bent back or weak legs. Of course, there can be some physical cause, but if you are sick all the time without any particular reason, it is possible that you are being possessed by animal spirits and the like.

At these times, please make an effort to purify your mind and make it as clear as a mirror. Just like wiping a mirror with a cloth, clean off your bad thoughts.

When your room is dirty and messy, other people will not come and clean it up for you. In fact, you probably will not allow them to enter your room and clean it without asking just because they want to. If you have made your room messy, dirty, and full of trash, it is your job to clean it up.

When cleaning up, a selfish person might open up the window and just throw out all the garbage from their house or their room onto the street. But it would surely draw complaints from their neighbors. Of course, this is not a good thing to do. You must know about this.

No matter how pretty someone looks, how nice their voice or how beautiful their outfit is, or how charming they are, you would feel disappointed if they have poor lifestyle habits. For example, you might overhear, "Apparently, she's quite messy. Her room is filled with trash, and she doesn't do laundry, so her underwear is left piling up for a month." Even if you are head over heels for her, you could be utterly discouraged upon hearing this. After all, we must do what we can for things we are responsible for.

A sloppy way of life would make others think you are unworthy of being given a certain position or prevent your work from going well. But you, yourself, may not know why and complain: "Why not me?" "Why am I not chosen?" You may have a negative reputation because of your poor day-to-day lifestyle, so please be careful.

This concludes my lecture on "Curses, Spells, and Possession."

CHAPTER FOUR

The Fight against Devils

—Revealing the Reality of Devils
and Their Tactics

1

Historically, Religions Have Fought against Devils

Devils target those with strong influential power

One of the topics I cannot avoid when teaching about hell or preaching the laws of hell is encounters with devils. The number of devils is limited so they do not possess just anyone. So actually, ordinary people can live their lives without experiencing a fight against devils. When devils possess someone, they usually have a goal. For instance, they would try and destroy the life of someone they think will enable them to fulfill their big goal by possessing them.

In hell, devils in fact work like mafia bosses; they use their henchmen to try and drag down other souls into still deeper levels of hell. But, as I said, their number is limited so there are not very many of them.

The Vatican uses something like an encyclopedia of devils when training exorcists-to-be. These trainees are shown the drawings and names of devils and are told to memorize their appearances, characteristics, and names. I am not sure of the details because I have never received training at the Vatican, but I have heard that the trainees have to memorize the faces and names of about 500 different devils.

There are pros and cons to this. If you know devils' names, they may use the name and appear before you, or you might attract them yourself. Therefore, I myself reveal only a few devil's names. If I reveal more, it would only allow numerous devils to take it as an advantage to approach you or deceive you.

In general, people are more likely to be possessed by lost spirits wandering on earth, but if the powerful devils see that they could exert significant influence through the work that you do, they might target you. But for such a thing to happen, you are most likely to have attracted four, five, or six evil spirits already.

Devils are often found within religious organizations that are wrong or absurd as a religion. These organizations have become like "evil spirits–producing factories," so many devils can be found there.

There are different levels of devils: low-level devils, moderately strong devils, and powerful devils. Some of them act arrogant for having henchmen and claim to be the "king of demons."

In this way, devils are more difficult to handle than normal evil spirits. The spirits that possess ordinary people are usually the spirits of their ancestors, a lost spirit haunting a certain place, or a spirit possessing someone whom they just happened to meet. But devils are on a different level compared with those spirits.

Oftentimes, Happy Science movies depict attacks by devils, but please do not think, "I've been possessed by a devil so I must be an important person." Nothing good comes out of thinking like this and being arrogant, so I do not recommend it. When you are possessed by a devil, unlike ordinary evil spirits, it cannot easily be sent to heaven or expelled. Devils are very skillful in deceiving people and are more cunning, so they are very difficult to deal with.

In some cases, devils may even appear while calling themselves angels, God, or Buddha. They also prey on religious seekers who are training in the mountains or forests. They like to disturb people who are seeking the Path. That is why they are often watching out for the chance to make an appearance when seekers are about to reach a higher level of awareness and be able to guide a large number of people or acquire Dharma power.

As I have mentioned in the beginning, devils often have a goal; hence, they are different from the ordinary spirits that you happen to walk by or spirits haunting a certain place. Devils are beings that persistently go after their target and scheme all kinds of plots to fulfill the goal.

So, if a devil comes when a person with spiritual power conducts spiritual phenomena, it can disguise itself in various forms and lie about its identity by saying different names. They occasionally appear in Happy Science, too, and my disciples sometimes get tricked by them. So we must be careful of these things.

How devils in hell came into being

Let me reorganize the key points. Close to this earthly world, there is an area that is a part of the other world inhabited by lost spirits. Far above it is heaven or the heavenly world. There is also the world of hell that is commonly understood as the underground world. It is a dark world, where sunlight does not reach.

There are different levels to hell as well. Most part of the shallow area of hell is dark or dim, like how it is in the evening. But when you go deeper and deeper, it gets so dark to the point you cannot see anything. The deepest level of hell is pitch-black as if coal tar is poured in. In short, there are different levels of darkness in hell.

Now, what makes devils different from evil spirits? In most cases, it takes many more years for a spirit to become a devil. Most devils were previously humans who fell to hell. In some cases, as spirits spend 500–1,000 years there, they become devils. Because they are unable to return to heaven or be reincarnated on earth, they continue to do evil and this turns them into devils.

This is something understandable. Anyone who hangs out with delinquents or works with gangsters for a long time will gradually look the part. It works in the same way.

However, when we trace back to the origin of devils, we see that most of them used to be angels or archangels. Eons ago, they rebelled against or grew jealous of God, fell from grace, and could no longer return to the heavenly world. They then became kings of hell or emperors of hell and formed their own world. In a sense, hell can be likened to the world of mafia.

At times, devils use their henchmen and form a team, but they do not usually fight together or help each other. This is, in a way, good for us. It would be quite troublesome if tens or hundreds of devils came to attack us all at once. But in reality, they do not get along with each other very well. Therefore, all they have to rely on is themselves or their own henchmen, at most.

The Christian ideas of purgatory and hell show how small-minded human beings can be

There are different lineages of devils, and they choose their target accordingly. For example, there are Christian-related devils in Christianity, Muslim-related devils in Islam, Buddhist-related devils in Buddhism, and Shinto-related devils in Japanese Shinto. Like so, there are devils in connection to each ethnicity and religion.

In the cases of Japanese religions, many of them do not clearly acknowledge the existence of devils. Japanese people often worship spirits with a superpower or psychic power as if they are gods, so I am afraid that Japanese religions are poor at distinguishing between good and evil on these matters. Perhaps this suggests that Japan did not have many significant religious leaders or that it is relatively behind other races.

But neither can I say that Christianity has an in-depth understanding of hell. In the Bible, you will read Jesus saying something like, "You will fall to hell and be burned in the eternal fire." So an average Christian believes that once you fall to hell, you can never get out of it; you can never escape the spiritual, eternal fire that destroys the soul. Most of them think of hell as a very stereotypical place, like the Hell of Agonizing Cries.

The original Christian teachings say that the heavenly world exists and that hell is a world where you lose your eternal life once you have fallen there. They basically teach that those who have faith in Jesus and study and practice Jesus' teachings will gain eternal life.

According to the teachings of traditional Christian churches, you cannot pass through the gate of heaven unless you become a Christian. They probably said so partly for the purpose of doing missionary activities, but basically, it means that followers of other religions will all go to hell. I understand they were saying that for missionary purposes and to convert people to Christianity. It may have been acceptable in terms of spreading the religion, but it would be too extreme to say that those who do not believe in Christianity will all fall to hell.

In the past, Julius Caesar traveled to Gaul—which is now the area around France and Germany—in an expedition to Europe. Some of their armies crossed over to England on a boat. Afterward, when they occupied many European areas, they sent over Christian missionaries and encouraged people in those colonized areas to believe in their religion. But in most cases, those people already had faith in a sort of religion that offered some kind of ceremonial service for their ancestors. So when they were told that one cannot return to heaven unless they believe in Christianity, they asked, "We have a chance to convert to Christianity, but what about our parents, grandparents, or ancestors? What was the meaning of all our rituals for ancestors?" Christianity was troubled by such questions.

If all non-Christians fall to hell and are burned in the eternal fire, it means people only started to enter heaven 2,000 years ago, and those who came before Christianity started are all in hell. Objectively, it is a rather one-sided logic.

To solve that issue, Christianity came up with the intermediate place called "purgatory." Simply put, this is a place where the souls of those who were alive without encountering Christianity reside; once they have repented and pledged devotion to the Christian teachings, they can ascend to heaven from there and even be reborn as humans. They put forth the concept of purgatory as an intermediate place located above hell.

Around 1300 AD, Dante Alighieri of Italy wrote a narrative poem titled *The Divine Comedy*, which comprises three major sections: Inferno (hell), Purgatorio (purgatory), and Paradiso (heaven). It has clear descriptions of each world, so the distinction between these worlds became more apparent around the Middle Ages. Before that, most Christians probably believed that those who were not Christians would all go straight to hell.

In the fourth century AD, Saint Augustine parted from Christianity and deeply immersed in Manichaeism. At the time, his mother Monica worked extremely hard to bring him back and he converted back to Christianity. She tried very hard to convince him because she believed that non-Christians would go to hell.

In reality, as written in Happy Science books such as *The Laws of the Sun*, *The Golden Laws*, and *The Laws of Eternity*, Buddha, God, or those representing Buddha and

God have been born on earth and taught religious teachings that were necessary for the time and region. Angels of light, bodhisattvas, and tathagatas have been born on earth as well. Even though their teachings may be of different types, if the teachings befit the time and region, then they can save people. Not being able to understand this shows how narrow-minded human beings are.

I understand why Christianity took such an approach. It is the same as how you would feel when you run a shop and a similar one opens next door. You would not like it if another liquor shop opens next to your own one or another grocery shop opens next to your own one. It is slightly similar to that.

Today, however, there are streets where similar shops are gathered together. A lot of people gather around such streets, and there are plenty of customers. In Tokyo, for example, there are particular areas with many *okonomiyaki* (Japanese savory pancakes) or *oden* (Japanese hot-pot dish) restaurants. There are also streets with many bars. In these areas, you can freely choose which restaurant to eat at; thus, many people casually come by without having any specific plan. When you say, "Let's go to Tsukishima for *monjayaki* (Japanese pan-fried batter similar to okonomiyaki)," you don't need to have a particular restaurant in mind. You just go there and browse for the one you want to eat at—somewhere that is not crowded but has delicious food and a good atmosphere. This is possible now, but it must have been very troublesome back then to have others "running the same business" as yours near you.

Hell and devils that were born as a result of the wars between Christianity and Islam

Hatred, such as the one I just mentioned, was what led Christians to fight Muslims over the Holy Land—in other words, the Crusades to Jerusalem. They fought in three major wars. The Christian side dispatched their army from Europe to attack and get Jerusalem back. During the Crusades, horrendous battles took place and the territorial power swayed back and forth, with both sides suffering immense casualties. Nevertheless, Christians were not able to take back Jerusalem for long. Numerous war heroes also appeared, but I must say, those wars were put forth partly out of ignorance.

One of the kings from Romania during the Crusades was Vlad Dracula, who later became the model for the legend of Count Dracula as we now know it. I assume he was strong, and he did things like chopping off the enemy's head and staking it on a stick for display. This must have been an extremely unbearable sight. In most cases, his enemies were Muslims. The scene was surely hell.

In this way, hell and devils can make their appearance on either side of the party, so this is a difficult point. You could go to hell and turn into a devil in exchange for your status, power, and fame in this earthly world.

Some might think it would be fun to be a devil because you can order people around, manipulate other people's souls at will, and possess people on earth and make them suffer. This could be one way of looking at it but just think about it. Suppose you are in an amusement park such as Disneyland. Being a devil is like forever playing the role of a ghost in a haunted house or forever riding on a roller coaster. I don't think it would be much fun at all.

2

The Deepest Pits of Hell You Never Knew

Sixteen major hells that await materialists after death

One element of hell is, indeed, fear. In addition to fear, there are feelings of pain, suffering, and sadness. These feelings can be experienced in the human world as well, but in the world of hell, they exist in their extreme form.

After all, most of those who are in hell have the same mindset as the so-called materialists who are currently living in this world—the people who believe that only material things exist and that this world is all there is or that life is finite.

These kinds of people often end up in hell, and in most cases, what awaits them is the kind of torture they would rather not go through. When you think of yourself as mere physical existence, what would be the most terrible, painful, and saddening thing that could happen to you? It would be, for example, suffering from the pain of being slashed or shot. That is one type of suffering. In this way, there is a kind of hell where you would suffer from physical pain, over and over again, by being chased by someone with a knife, being slashed or shot, or jumping off from a high place to your death.

Another kind of hell is, as I previously mentioned, the Hell of Agonizing Cries—a torturous place in which you would want to cry and scream. There is such a hell.

There are also realms of hell that are associated with country and region. The ones that have been handed down in Japan are called the Eight Major Hells: eight types of both Scorching Hells and Freezing Hells.

These hells differ depending on the region. Japan has both summer and winter, so, understandably, there are both Scorching Hells and Freezing Hells. But I do not think there are Freezing Hells in extremely hot areas or something like Burning Hells in extremely cold areas. It is all based on region.

In Japan, there are sixteen major hells—eight Freezing Hells and eight Scorching Hells. This concept also came from China and nearby areas, so I presume these hells exist there, too, although, perhaps things are a little different further north.

Scorching Hells mostly exist in countries or regions with many volcanoes, whereas Freezing Hells often appear in areas with heavy snow or where people often die in ice-related accidents. That is how it is. Both the scorching hotness and the subzero coldness endanger the lives of those living on earth. Therefore, these hells are, without a doubt, fearful to those who think that their lives are only of physical matter.

Subzero temperatures you experience in Japan would be minus two or three degree Celsius (26–28 °F) in general; it gets a little lower in Hokkaido. In New York, it sometimes reaches around minus 20 degree Celsius (−4 °F) even without snow. Although New York is at a similar latitude as the Aomori Prefecture of Japan, it is colder. A coat is not enough to keep you warm. My cotton coat that I wore in Japan was not enough to keep me warm in a temperature of minus 20 degree Celsius. It is freezing without a little expensive cashmere coat. Down coats did not exist back when I was living in New York, but they began circulating in later years. These can also protect you from the cold.

In any case, Freezing Hells and Scorching Hells really do exist, and you do not know which hell you might end up in. It also depends on how you lived your life. Those burning with jealousy or those with strong hatred, envy, or grudge often end up in Scorching Hells. On the other hand, Freezing Hells are mostly related to loneliness, fear, and poverty. Food shortage is another major reason.

Being in hell means you are already a spirit body, so in many cases, your appearance will gradually change into a form that suits the environment. There, you will experience things that you would hate to experience on earth, over and over again.

You may have seen various illustrations of hell. Some of them are a little exaggerated, whereas others are not. In Christianity, Dante Alighieri depicted heaven, purgatory, and hell. When I read his depiction of purgatory, I found it a little obscure and unclear. I assume that a large part of it was made up from his imagination. Many famous historical figures appear in the section about heaven, whereas those who were referred to as being atrocious and inhumane appear in the section about hell. Kings and religious leaders of other races also appear in hell. But I have to say that he did not necessarily write it for the sake of depicting the Spirit World.

The types of people who
fall straight to the Abysmal Hell

Speaking of purgatory (*rengoku* [煉獄] in Japanese), there is a character called Kyojuro Rengoku in the anime *Demon Slayer*, which became popular in Japan and around the world. He is a very strong 20-year-old demon slayer known as *Hashira*, the leader of those who fight demons. I thought, "What a name to give a character." I guess children do not understand what his name means, but such a character appears in the anime. Anyway, Christianity has the concept of purgatory.

In Japan, on the other hand, people are not very familiar with purgatory. According to the understanding of most Japanese people, what Jesus meant by "falling to hell and losing your eternal life" or "the hell you can never escape from" are places where the so-called satans and devils reside. Such hell is inhabited by those who have truly turned into devils and become the "missionary squad of hell," who are scheming all kinds of plots to expand the forces in hell. In general, these beings cannot get out of there.

There are also the types of people who fall straight to the pits of hell called the Abysmal Hell. They fall there headfirst, and in many cases, they cannot get out of it so easily. The majority of people who fall to the bottomless Abysmal Hell are philosophers, scholars, politicians, and others who had a strong power of influence.

Take philosophers, for example: they have not necessarily committed crimes in the worldly sense, but they have "poured poisonous thoughts into people's minds." Because the thoughts influenced too many people, some of them cannot get out of this hell. They might have been in a respectable position to guide others in this world, and they might have had status or been rich.

I do not want to mention specific names, but if I were to give you a few examples, among them are people who write many novels or make many movies about gruesome crimes. These people are intrigued by hellish matters, so their minds are attuned to hell. Then, when they die, they fall straight to hell without even receiving the judgment of Yama. In many cases, they are not granted a chance to watch their lives on a Life-Reflecting Mirror, or *johari no kagami* (Yama's crystal-clear mirror), and to reflect on themselves; they fall headfirst to hell.

Among scholars of liberal arts are many who specialize in philosophy and religious studies; they, too, may have to spend a certain period in hell first. In most cases, it is because they have become agitators or spreaders of hellish ideas. Many of them were regarded as great professors in this world. Even a professor emeritus at the University of Tokyo has gone to the Abysmal Hell and so has a renowned author.

It is indeed very difficult to tell whether a piece of work is heavenly or hellish. In a novel, for example, a character might be killed, but the question is whether the story as a whole has the power to convert or purify the readers' minds or if it is full of temptation to lead them toward hell or evil. Another point is whether the novel will make this earthly world better or worse.

Some works affirm materialism or are strongly tinted with revolutionary ideas that affirm killing, such as "There's no problem in killing people because humans are just materialistic beings." Furthermore, there may be other works that contribute to the spread of terribly cruel ideas. Authors of these works will fall to the Abysmal Hell, and when their sin is too heavy, they can even turn into devils. This is what has actually happened.

The sin of Nietzsche: Criticizing Christianity with *Übermensch* theory

As I wanted to talk about the fight against devils in hell in this chapter, I was reading some books related to this topic. Since two or three days ago, I have been reading a book by the German philosopher Nietzsche, who was also portrayed in the Happy Science movie, *The Laws of Eternity*. In my case, authors always spiritually appear before me when I read their books. They are quite persistent and troublesome. The philosophical idea written in the book I was reading was the Superman (*Übermensch*) theory that criticized Christianity. Nietzsche also wrote the famous quote, "God is dead."

Nietzsche was born into a Protestant family, and his father was a pastor. He started to display his talent from around the age of 13, and I presume he was a smart, bright boy. He studied classical philology and was offered a position at the University of Basel when he was 24, and he became a professor at age 25. He must have been incredibly smart to become a professor of classical philology at such an age.

Nietzsche could read Greek, Latin, and other languages. He was meticulous and probably studied philosophies of the past as well. This proves that being smart does not necessarily mean you will go to the heavenly world after death. Although he became a professor at age 25, the philosophies he presented were extremely heretical, so he drew floods of criticism, which eventually drove him out of the academic world.

His famous work is *Thus Spoke Zarathustra*, and there is a classical music piece with the same title. Zarathustra refers to Zoroaster. Nietzsche thought, "Jesus was made into a criminal and was crucified alongside other criminals. He was nailed to the cross, his legs were broken, he was pierced by a spear, and he died. In the earthly sense, he was a weak god." He then concluded that it was ridiculous to believe in such a man. He also said that Jesus was killed by the *ressentiment* of the Jewish people. Ressentiment means something like a mass of jealousy. He saw Jesus as a god who was killed by people's jealousy.

What is more, he thought, "After Jesus was crucified, the crucifix was made into a symbol of God. Christians used it to say that humanity was saved by Jesus' crucifixion. This idea started with Paul the Apostle and was spread by others. They made this idea up to make a weak person who was killed in this world be regarded as a great person. So Christianity is almost like fraud." This is one of the weak points of Christianity that he spotted and attacked.

His father was in his 30s when he died, so I do not know how much Nietzsche was influenced by his family, but I am sure he knew a lot about Christian doctrine, as he was the son of a pastor. He thought it was stupid how everyone worshiped such a weak god, and he thought that a real god must be strong.

In Japan, vengeful spirits are enshrined to prevent them from cursing people

A similar view exists in Japan as well. Those referred to as gods in Japan are usually war gods; the winners of the war were often enshrined as gods. But when people feared that the ones on the losing side would become vengeful spirits, they built a mausoleum or shrine to revere them as "gods," also. Because people feared their curses, they gave them "god" status and offerings. In this way, people tried to keep those spirits from cursing.

One of the famous examples of this is Sugawara no Michizane (845-903) of Dazaifu Tenmangu Shrine, now known as the god of learning. He was a politician but was demoted and exiled to Dazaifu in Kyushu. He is also famous for abolishing the Japanese missions to Tang China. He was very smart but was still exiled.

Another example is Taira no Masakado (ca. 903–940), who is famous for his rebellion against the imperial court. He raised an army in the Kanto region and started a rebellion.

Decades ago, the Long-Term Credit Bank of Japan—which now has a different name—was headquartered in Chiyoda Ward in Tokyo. It had a black building that was very dark and spooky, but it was well-received by the people. It was a tall, long building with an unusual design; about halfway up, both sides of the building were carved out in a horizontal U-shape, and the building continued up to the top. On seeing this, I was worried that it might collapse during an earthquake. In one corner of its premises, there was a tomb that enshrined the decapitated head of Taira no Masakado.

Everyone at the bank feared this corner and avoided sitting with their back against the tomb. But as expected, mysterious deaths occurred, one after another, to those who sat facing away from the tomb. The incidents were even reported in the newspapers, so people were fearful of the tomb. I think the building was later rebuilt, but this must have been scary. It is scary how someone is still giving out curses even after 1,000 years.

Speaking of Taira no Masakado, I had the following experience. When the Happy Science headquarters was located in Kioicho Building near Akasaka, I met Haruki Kadokawa of Kadokawa Shoten Publishing. He was quite an eccentric man; he built a Kadokawa shrine and made himself its priest. He claimed to be a psychic and also made movies that dealt with supernatural power or the spiritual world from time to time. Such a person gave us offers to publish pocket-sized paperback books, so we published around 10 books from his company, including *The Laws of the Sun*, *The Golden Laws*, and *The Laws of Eternity*. That is why he sometimes visited our headquarters.

One day, he asked me, "Who do you think I was in my past life? Please tell me your judgment." I replied, "I'm sure you've heard it from other psychics. Maybe I shouldn't say it." But he insisted, "No, I haven't heard anything, so please." I knew he went to other psychics and was told that his past life was a Japanese feudal lord Takeda Shingen. That is why he was behaving like a samurai general of the Warring States Period, believing himself to be fighting to "take over Japan." But in my eyes, he was obviously Taira no Masakado.

The spirit of Taira no Masakado was always with him, so I thought that his life must have been difficult and would be troublesome in the future. The movies from Kadokawa Pictures back then were often things like *Samurai Reincarnation* and *Tokyo: The Last War*. Indeed, they depicted a demonic world; the stories were exactly about the world of demons. So I told him, "You might have been Taira no

Masakado in your past life, but you were probably told something different by other psychics." But I do not know whether he believed me or not.

Given that I was a psychic, he would open his heart and tell me various things without any concern. He once mentioned how someone had told him, "Do you remember the volcanic eruption that occurred in South America the other day? I guess it's you, Mr. Kadokawa, who made it happen." I just listened to him and said, "Oh, is that so?" But for someone running a top-tier company, he was saying risky things.

When I was speaking to him back then, I felt light-headed, and it seemed as if the space around me was being distorted. I used to wonder what this phenomenon was. When he was arrested sometime later and convicted of possessing illegal drugs, I understood that the feeling of space distorting and my head spinning was a reflection of his drug use. So he was having a "trip." Perhaps he visited the other world and got ideas from it for his creative work.

During those years, in summer, I would often rent a log cabin or a cottage in Karuizawa and seclude myself there. I think it was in the evening of the day when Mr. Kadokawa's arrest aired on the news; I saw a black shadow of someone sitting with his knees to his chest in the corner of the living room. At the time, I had not watched the news, so I did not know about his arrest.

I thought, "What's that? A black thing is sitting in the corner of the room." I closely looked at it and saw how it very much resembled Mr. Haruki Kadokawa. I wondered what it meant and why he was there. Oftentimes, when someone dies, their spirit visits me, so I thought he had died. But that was not the case. Afterward, I saw Mr. Kadokawa's arrest on the news and thought, "Oh, perhaps he came here to ask me for help."

At another time, I also heard that when he was undergoing an operation for cancer or something, he was listening to *The True Words Spoken By Buddha* on his headphones nonstop while being bedridden. So he probably trusted me as a psychic. Apparently, he then recovered from that illness.

There are various types of psychics, so we must see through what kind of beings and what kind of world these psychics are connected to.

The True Words Spoken By Buddha,
the fundamental sutra of Happy Science (see p.258).

3

Even Now,
Devils Haunt Certain Religions

The danger of psychic-power worship
lying in evil psychic religions

Especially, we must be wary of evil religious groups that focus on psychic power. If you have been involved with them for years, you will be possessed by the evil spirits that inhabit those groups. These evil spirits cannot be easily expelled, and this is a very serious problem.

As for the groups of esoteric Shingon Buddhism, some are orthodox and good, but others focus on the practice of putting a death spell on a target person. There are also groups that teach their believers to cast their hands over another person to purify and expel evil spirits, even though they themselves have not attained enlightenment. Many of these groups are wrong; not only do hellish spirits flock to these groups, but some are even guided by devils. There are many members who belong to these groups and practice such rituals, so this is a big issue.

At Happy Science, too, we had some staff who used to be long-time believers of these religious groups. One of them was living within their institution and took their seminars. But if you belonged to a certain group for a long time, it becomes very difficult to remove the possessing spirits you previously attuned to. Those who were devout believers and practiced their faith 24/7 in the institution will find it especially difficult to expel the possessing spirits. Even after becoming a renunciant disciple of Happy Science, that person was unfortunately dragged back into the old nest.

Even in psychic-power worship, there should be rightful teaching. People should correct their own actions by self-reflection and should improve their character as human beings. Therefore, the groups advocating that all problems will be solved by supernatural powers are indeed dangerous. I came to understand this as I went through various experiences.

There is even a group that teaches that by casting your hand over a person, you can remove the evil spirits possessing him or her as if removing layers of thin paper. They encourage their members—who are possessed by stray spirits—to practice it with one another. Even if I tell them, "Logically, that's impossible. How can you expel evil spirits when you don't have the power to send God's light into the other person?" they will say, "Yes, we can. We are wearing a spiritual ornament called *omitama*, so we can expel evil spirits." This is a group related to the Mahikari (lit. true light) religion.

I actually experienced the purification ritual of a Mahikari-related religious group. It was around the time I started communicating with the Spirit World. I attended an 18-day driver's education boot camp held at Higashi Ashikaga Driving School in Tochigi Prefecture. Among the people I spent those days with, there was a young person who was a member of a group practicing Mahikari. As I conversed with him, we ended up talking about religion.

This group has a sutra or a type of Shinto prayer called *norito*, which is often recited by Shinto-related religions. They use the sutra or norito of the same content, which starts by saying, "The names of gods residing in Takamanohara are..." The group the person belonged to would pronounce it "Takamanohara" instead of "Takamagahara." They would wear a pendant called *omitama*, which is similar to a comma-shaped bead, and cast their hand over you while reciting the prayer.

My spiritual channel was already open by then. To describe how I felt while receiving this ritual, I actually felt sizzling hot. While the person was casting his hand over me, I felt as if I was being grilled. It was not the kind of warmth that flows from heaven; it was a sizzling, burning sensation. The believers of the group he belonged to probably think of it as God's light, but from what I felt, it is what you would feel in the Hell of Scorching Heat or the Hell of Great Scorching Heat.

In fact, the founder of this religious group has fallen to this hell. While he was alive, he would often say things like, "The rain of fire will pour!" "The Apocalypse will come, and the rain of fire will fall." Indeed, I felt such blazing heat. That was the Hell of Scorching Heat. This kind of thing can happen.

The difference in "guidance" between the spirits in heaven and the devils in hell

Some religions or faiths can make you feel a sizzling heat, whereas others can make you feel a shivering coldness. In fact, there are relatively many religions that give you the chills and make you shudder. Sometimes, you become cold, as if the temperature has dropped. This not only occurs with devils but also with the spirits from hell in general. It is practically the same phenomenon you experience at a haunted house.

Let me share my own experience concerning this. I already mentioned this long ago, but it was when my elder brother was still alive. His spiritual channel was also open, so although I felt bad for him, I always asked him to be a medium to channel the evil spirits, whereas I only channeled the light of angels when giving spiritual messages. Nowadays, I have to channel both of them, so it has become a hassle, but back then, my brother used to be the "expert" at channeling evil spirits.

My parents' house in Kawashima Town (Yoshinogawa City) had three rooms on the second floor, and we used to use the middle room to conduct spiritual messages. While we were receiving messages from an evil spirit, the room temperature dropped by two degree Celsius. We felt cold, and the temperature actually dropped on the thermometer too, so I learned that evil spirits really do make the temperature drop.

If you practice spiritual discipline or experience spiritual phenomena and you often feel extremely cold or unbearably hot—as if being burned, grilled on an iron plate, or being boiled in a pot—you must suspect that something unheavenly has come to you.

However, if a heavenly spirit has come down to you when you are possessed by an evil spirit, you will feel as if something was suddenly peeled away from you. Metaphorically, it is similar to when wallpaper is peeled off a wall. Then you will feel some warmth and be at peace.

In contrast, when a devil comes, you will feel something very heavy in your stomach, as if an iron ball is placed there. You will get a dull stomachache. I have heard that other people also experienced this; now, let me share my own experience.

There is a religious group called GLA in Japan, which split off into various factions after the death of its founder, Shinji Takahashi. One of the faction leaders was Yuko Chino, who has already passed away. She published numerous books that all had similar titles. The contents of those books are not so different from what Shinji Takahashi used to write.

My father and elder brother read her books, but they could not tell whether they were heavenly or hellish. They sent one of her books to me, saying, "I think it's a good book. It talks about love and mercy. It is published by Mercy and Love Publishing, so it must contain good things." When I read it, even before reaching halfway through the book, I could not continue; the words started to flicker and my stomach felt tremendously heavy. I could not stand it nor could I even keep the book in my room, so I had no choice but to discard it, though I mean no offense to the author.

If you have ever belonged to some religious group that is controlled by evil spirits and have many of their books, I recommend that you do not keep them in your room. You can be connected to spirits of the same kind even through books.

What about my books? When I was still working at a Japanese trading company, I published the fifth book of my spiritual message series, *Spiritual Messages from Socrates*.

I went to the biggest bookstore in Nagoya—I think it was Maruzen—on my lunch break to see how they were piled up on display. Then I saw golden light being emitted from the stack of my books. I was so surprised to see that. It was as if rows of golden "lunch boxes" were stacked up in great numbers. It was the first time I perceived the light that shines forth from the books of Truth so clearly.

Books that emit light and books that give off hellish vibrations are lined up next to each other in bookstores. Some people buy them without being aware of that, and some are drawn to things that are not good. You should be careful about this point.

The problems of the Unification Church

Another problem is with the Unification Church. In a way, it started by advocating a similar narrative to Happy Science. They claim that their founder, Sun Myung Moon—who has already passed away—was the Second Coming of Jesus Christ, whereas we say at Happy Science, "Ryuho Okawa is the Buddha Reborn," which sounds a little similar. Moreover, in the early days, I gave 10 lectures on the "principle series," and when those lectures were made into books, I was told by the publishing company, "If you say 'principle' too much, people might mistake you for that particular religious group. You may want to consider changing the title."

The Unification Church practically has no books on its basic teachings. *Divine Principle* is the only one, and it covers their main teachings. It starts with the story of Adam and Eve and describes how Eve fell into the temptation of Satan, leading to Adam's corruption. So it is based on a theory of degradation—how humanity on earth became corrupt. It then says, "People must go back to heaven or to Eden, and that's why we must do missionary work." This is what *Divine Principle* teaches.

In this book, it is written that "Japan is Eve and South Korea is Adam. The devil made its way into Japan, or Eve, and seduced South Korea into becoming the horrible state it is in today." This idea is well-received in South Korea and they continue to advocate the idea, "Japan is inherently evil."

Koreans are endlessly talking about what happened 100 years ago. Even today, some Koreans say, for example, "I was forced to work for a heavy industry company of a certain Japanese conglomerate before World War II," demanding Japan to pay them compensation. This is a mentality that underlies South Korean people.

In other words, the view of the Unification Church can be summarized as this: "Koreans were deceived by Eve or Japan. Satan possessed Japan, and they deceived us and ruined the Korean peninsula. Japan will only be forgiven when it suffers and repents for its sins. Thus, Japanese women are equivalent to animals. Since Japanese women are the same as beasts, it won't be a sin to bring any of them over to Korea for a mass wedding."

They then teach, "Since Japan is Eve, it is a good thing to suck money out of it. Take as much money as you can from Japan and bring it to South Korea." They practically have nothing to teach or sell, so in the end, the founder would tell his members to turn even stones into money by selling them. It saddens me how, sometimes, young Japanese girls have to sell carnations for money, like flower girls, at a traffic intersection. They sell flowers in dangerous spots where they could get caught up in an accident. There seems to be an order that says: "Use whatever means to drain money from Japan as if sucking blood and send it to South Korea!"

By making Japan the enemy with this thinking, the Unification Church is aiming at dissolving the division with North Korea. They are saying, "Japan, the country of Eve, is our common enemy. Let's beat out the devil from Japan and save ourselves. Then we can all return to the Garden of Eden." That is why this religion has not been regarded so negatively in the Korean peninsula.

In Japan, they were heavily attacked by the mass media for having a too-close relationship with the Liberal Democratic Party (LDP). They have supported LDP during elections, provided them with secretaries, sent them money, and done various other things. This is nothing new; they try to get closer to key figures.

However, I feel sorry for their believers because many of them are pure in their hearts. It is truly unfortunate, and I feel very sad about that. Their members are told to get closer to not only politicians but also other people; Professor Shoichi Watanabe, a well-known scholar and critic, had a maid who was a member of the Unification Church. He had three young children at the time, so he needed someone to take care of the house.

This maid was in her late teens when she started to work at his house, and she worked there for almost 10 years. According to Mr. Watanabe, she was a very dedicated girl. He described her saying, "She worked very hard. She was the kind of girl who would take her meals alone when no one was around and eat a very small portion as if biting on a tiny cookie. For us, she was very helpful." She worked there until Mr. Watanabe's children entered middle school. Because the Unification Church runs the International Federation for Victory Over Communism, I assume when they find some key figures whom they feel they could "use," they dispatch their members to them.

I am sure they do this to politicians as well. The number of state-funded secretaries per Diet member is determined by the Diet Act, so they send additional secretaries to some politicians to help with their work. I think that is what they do. Their members are doing so thinking that they are doing something good, and many of them actually seem pure and innocent.

When I was in the United States, I was stopped by one of their members at a street corner in Manhattan. I did not know their English group name back then. A lady who could speak a little Japanese mentioned "intellect, emotion, volition" in Japanese. I thought to myself, "What! Why on earth does an American person know these Japanese words?" Anyhow, she invited me to their gathering for a conversation.

I do not remember whether it was Friday or Saturday evening. She told me, "We have an evening gathering; we just get together, have a light dinner, and chat. We are Christians." I thought it would not be bad to study Christianity. In the middle of Manhattan—I think it was near 50th Street—I was told that "intellect, emotion, volition" are important. So I followed her without any suspicion and joined the gathering.

When I went inside, another person—a chef of Japanese cuisine who was studying in the United States—was also "captured" there, so the two of us were targeted. I think I was conversing with them for about five hours. We started in the early evening and continued for five hours. I thought this would never end, so I unveiled myself, put on an "armor," and told them, "I also have spiritual power. I know spiritual matters." When I showed them a spiritual practice and spoke in an unknown language, they seemed irritated and said, "We know, we know that too"—they suddenly changed their attitude. While I was speaking with them, the chef ran away, and I was left to deal with them alone.

I was asked to write my address, name, and phone number, but I thought it might be risky. So I just wrote my address and not my phone number. Later on, I often received postcards from them, but I did not go back there since then.

The people I met did seem kind. They seemed kind and very friendly at a glance, and because they mentioned things like, "All religions must become one," it sounded like they were saying good things. But they approach you using various means that are almost like fraud. For example, they would start with things like palmistry. A Japanese lady who was at the gathering also did things like palmistry and said to me, "You are an intelligent man." But she probably said the same thing to everyone. People who are working for a Japanese company and are sent to New York are mostly elites. That is why, in most cases, it would not be wrong by saying, "You are an intelligent person." She would start by flattering you to entrap you in this way. She seemed friendly and kind, and although I felt sorry for her, there was not much I could do.

In the case of the Unification Church, you will not feel "sizzling heat" or "frigid coldness." At a glance, their approach is soft and gentle, but it feels as if you are slowly being tangled up by a spider's web until you are captured in their nest. Once you are tangled up and captured in their nest, a "spider" will swiftly appear, and you will be completely seized. This is how they do things.

In both religion and politics, you need the right purpose, motive, means, process, and results

So why is the Unification Church wrong? Let us look at an incident, for example. They formed a Buddhist group in Hokkaido under a different name, made things like prayer beads and pots, and sold them at a high price; this led them to be interrogated as an organization for committing spiritual fraud. In this way, this religion uses various kinds of fraudulent means—using fake names, doing things like onomancy and palmistry, making all kinds of excuses, or taking a Buddhist approach—and they believe it is fine as long as they yield good results. This is where they are wrong.

Therefore, to think, "It's OK to deceive someone" is wrong. This is the point some people may find difficult to understand, but a good result is worth nothing if the means are bad.

This is true with communism, too. Take, for example, the revolution of Mao Zedong. He may seem like a hero when you focus on how he started a revolution to rule the entire nation and how he eventually built a great empire and restored China. However, it was nothing but an armed revolution. He said, "Political power grows out of the barrel of a gun," which means, "By killing people with a gun, a revolution arises and ends in success." It leads people to think, "It's OK to kill people. Use whatever means. As long as the result and purpose are right, anything is allowed." But within this attitude, there are many wrong ideas. Tens of millions of people starved to death during his revolution.

You must definitely have the right purpose, but you must also have the right means as well as the right motive. Happy Science must also have the right motive and create the right results using the right means.

Sometimes, illnesses are healed through miracles, but not everyone experiences that. So even promoting such miracles would be wrong if taken to the extreme.

A certain religious group (Seicho-no-Ie) used to sell themselves by saying that illnesses would heal just by reading their books. Sometimes, illnesses might heal, but other times, they will not. It is a blessing for miracles to happen, but you should not use these examples to mislead people.

The same can be said about donating money. It can be called in many ways, such as "contribution," "donation," or "offerings," and Happy Science calls it "happiness planting."

The very act of donating money for churches, shrines, and temples, for example, is a good deed. To begin with, Jesus was not good at making money, and Buddha did not encourage making money either. They lived off offerings and alms. The act of offering itself is a blessing and a precious deed.

But if you are collecting donations through wrongdoings or for wrong purposes, then you must reflect on that. That is where you need to check. Are your motives, means, processes, results, and purposes all consistent and righteous? You must check on this point. If many members of a certain religion end up going insane, then you must realize that there is something wrong with that group.

The mistaken thinking of "adverse destinies will naturally break away, and good results will follow"

One Japanese religious group claims that they can heal illnesses. Whenever a bad situation arises, they say things like, "Bad things are a sign of good things to come." A fever will go down once it rises, and by the same logic, they say, "You will soon get better." This group had split off from a religious group, Seicho-no-Ie. They first saw Happy Science on friendly terms, and they sometimes sent us their magazines. We then recorded spiritual messages from Masaharu Taniguchi, the founder of Seicho-no-Ie. In his spiritual messages, Masaharu Taniguchi said, "A former lecturer of Seicho-no-Ie, who used to give talks in a local region, went independent and founded his own group called Byakko Shinko Kai, but he is now in hell." The group got furious and cursed us: "Curse Masaharu Taniguchi and Ryuho Okawa. Go to hell." So they turned their back on us.

Many religions have similarities in their teachings to some extent. But if a religion only focuses on a certain teaching and misinterprets it, the religion can end up being in a helpless state.

The same problem arises with the Buddhist theory that says, "Amitabha Buddha places the salvation of bad people above the salvation of good people." Although it is true that bad people can be saved, it would be wrong to think, "The more evil you do, the more you will be saved."

Seicho-no-Ie teaches the "chemicalization of fate," which says, "When your bad fate falls apart, the situation may appear to worsen for a while, but after that, things will turn out for the better." This is a kind of positive thinking, but if misused, it can be used to justify everything. For example, if you are struggling at work, become ill, or have relationship problems, you can just say, "This is the process of my bad fate falling apart before everything becomes better. My fate is going through a chemicalization or catalysis, and that is why bad things are happening. From now on, it will only get better." But if you oversimplify things in this way, this idea can lead to mistakes.

In reality, you, yourself, might be the one causing your relationship problems. There might be a physical reason for your illness, and if so, you must treat it. A business failure is often a natural consequence in the eyes of a business expert. It may just be you who did not see it coming. That is why you should not attribute your misfortune to your fate; nor should you simply take it as your "bad karma falling apart."

4

Fighting against Devils Also Requires Using Worldly Common Sense and the Law of Causality

I have stepped into criticizing other religious groups, so there might be some problems. However, when speaking about the fight against devils, I cannot avoid pointing out the devils that nest in religious organizations.

Buddhist groups are no exception. For example, holding an ancestral memorial service is undoubtedly important, but it would be a lie to say things like, "As long as you hold ancestral memorial services, your destiny will improve and you will be saved from all your bad karmas." That is because you, yourself, might be creating the cause of your misfortune.

Some people blame everything on their parents or relatives and say, "I'm unhappy because the spirit of my father, mother, grandfather, or grandmother is lost and is unable to return to heaven. They are the very cause of all my miseries." In some cases, those spirits could truly be affecting your life. They could be haunting your house and possessing your family members. In some families, people die from the same cause for generations—for example, three generations dying in traffic accidents, in fire, or from cancer. Some religions take these incidents and say things like, "This is due to the karma of cancer" or "This is due to the karma of accidental deaths." They put all the blame on their ancestors in this way.

It is true that lost spirits often come relying on their descendants, but in terms of your own life, you must reflect on it yourself and correct what you can. Only when you attain the level of enlightenment where you emit light or a halo can you exert Dharma power to effectively conduct ancestral memorial service. Your light may be small, but by receiving that light, your ancestors will come to realize their mistakes.

It may also be important to go to those who undergo professional discipline and can truly exert spiritual power, and ask them to expel the lost spirits.

There are indeed many different teachings and methods. But it is true to say that those with a weak left brain, or who are a little weak in making worldly judgments, tend to go astray from the right path. So please be aware of that. You should have some knowledge regarding the common sense of this world, and you must also study the law of causality or the law of cause and effect.

This concludes the chapter.

CHAPTER FIVE

A Message from Savior

—Saving the Earth from Crisis

1

Earth Is in the Greatest Crisis in History

The COVID scare among humanity
and the dangers of an imminent major war

I have been speaking about the laws of hell, and in this last chapter, I would like to speak about what is on my mind as "A Message from Savior."

Now, Earth is in great crisis, and the severity of it is like never before.

When I first began this salvation movement, the population of the world was around five billion, but it is now already around eight billion. It means that Earth's population has grown by three billion people.

However, my teachings have not spread enough. They have not even reached the three billion people. Our salvation movement keeps seesawing, but looking at the current trend in the 2020s, I have to say the crisis humanity is facing is getting more serious.

One crisis is the spread of fear across humanity owing to the coronavirus pervading earth. Currently, about 700 million people have been infected by the virus, and a plethora of new variants are expected to spread. These viruses will be significant threats to humanity as a whole.

There are still people who do not believe that this pandemic was caused by a specific country. But let us say that the virus occurred naturally; I believe it is due to Earth Consciousness not being pleased with how the eight billion people are living on the surface of the Earth.

Another crisis is that the peaceful era, which has continued for about 80 years since the end of World War II, is coming to an end.

There were minor wars during these 80 years, but none of them led to a large-scale war that shook the entire world. However, the one that is about to happen would be fatal if we do not gather the wisdom of humanity to overcome it.

In general, when the population increases on earth, there is always a war. History shows that at such times food, energy, or resources become the reason for a war to happen. For example, wars break out even over water resources. Aside from water, conflicts can arise over grain, oil, coal, natural gas, nuclear power, and so on.

Although population increase may have some positive effects, it can give rise to a fierce battle between countries over those matters. As a consequence, this will inevitably cause countries to fight to expand their allies and eliminate their enemies. In terms of this, humanity must, from now on, learn from history and make use of the lessons from it. This is probably the only way to tackle this problem.

What would happen if the law becomes "God" and takes control

Another crisis is that the countries on earth are now split into several groups. What separates them are their ideologies, thoughts, or beliefs. According to what the United States is saying, the general understanding is that this is a battle between democracy and autocracy. But this idea that says, "the current democracy is just and autocracy is evil" is not correct. This is because there are issues on both sides.

Atheism and materialism are steadily spreading in democratic nations too. In other words, these nations are advocating scientism-oriented materialism, so their common grounds are the same as non-democratic nations.

Democracy is acceptable on the premise that people believe in God and proactively make decisions based on their good conscience as children of God. The same applies to law-abiding countries, which have developed using a democratic way of thinking: God's teachings must underlie their foundation as the nations "abide by the laws." However, now, humans have lost their faith and are not listening to God's teachings, so the laws are being made through discussions and votes of humans only. Therefore, the laws are "becoming God" and are controlling the world.

In addition, I am deeply concerned that more countries have adopted a surveillance system using artificial intelligence

(AI) and other means as their main tool to maintain their rule by law.

Of course, I am not opposed to utilizing machines and other technology to make our lives and society convenient. Essentially, the advancement of machinery must be the means to an end. However, it has now become the goal instead. Machinery has sadly become tools to control humans.

Machines are increasingly controlling people as the population increases. Now is an age when humans are ruled by the laws they have made themselves and are being monitored by AI and other machines. This means that, in a way, humans are becoming livestock.

There is another problem. Each country is sovereign to make its own laws based on the idea of the rule of law, and this tends to group the world into friend and foe. If countries are divided into friend and foe, the values of good and evil upheld by the rule of law on each side can often conflict with each other. Thus, if a country tries to apply the justice of their own country to the rest of the world, the act can be considered unjust to other nations. These types of issues have been occurring. Each country tends to only think about its nation when they create its law system, so the laws will not always agree with those of other nations.

This is a great crisis. The shortcomings in the modern political system or administration system that began in the 16th or 17th century are becoming more and more obvious.

In reality, there are countries that are trying to spread their domestic law system worldwide and are causing military or economic conflicts. While determining the tax rates is a country's sovereign matter, when it comes to deciding on the tax rates between countries, there should be negotiations and talks. But if any one nation has too strong an autocratic way of thinking, it will be difficult for countries to cooperate and have talks.

Thus, with the population increase, the number of conflicts will increase between countries. To solve these conflicts, each country will expand its military strength. There will also be competition to expand economic power.

In most cases, a country that has expanded military and economic power will harbor aggressive ways of thinking and begin taking over the weaker and smaller neighboring countries. On top of that, the country will start building an alliance or a union with other countries that uphold similar views and try to initiate a clash between groups of even larger countries. These cases have occurred in the past, although not exactly in the same way as what is happening now.

The most concerning issue now is that nuclear weapons really exist on Earth; permanent members of the United Nations Security Council and several other countries possess them. There is also a possibility that more countries will come to possess these weapons.

The problem with nuclear weapons is that they can override the rule of law and democracy and change the power relationship between countries. For example, if a country with only 20 million people is equipped with nuclear weapons that can be used to attack other countries, it could one-sidedly gain the upper hand over other nuclear-free countries that have a population of 100 million, 300 million, or even a billion people. The nuclear weapon itself is another power that overrides the system of democracy or the rule of law. Humanity is now being tested to see if their wisdom can resolve this issue.

Furthermore, owing to population increase, even the modern political systems that have been commonly adopted in developed countries—democracy, the rule of law, and the parliamentary system—no longer work without relying on the mass media; they have no choice but to rely on it to gain information and make decisions. But how does the mass media judge what is right? What are they trying to promote, and what are they trying to prevent? Their standard of right and wrong is only based on the corporate way of thinking, and this is becoming the power to fuel conflicts between countries.

Today, the voice of God and Buddha are not reaching the mass media. We have entered such an age.

2

We Must Not Allow Earth to Become Devils' Planet

This world is being allowed to exist as a school for soul training

In this modern world full of problems, what should we do? How should we go about it, and what outcome should we produce? We have several options, but to state the conclusion first, regardless of which option we choose, we might have to face harsh outcomes.

It is essentially difficult to teach what is right to the eight billion people who have neglected to consider the most basic premise: This world is merely a school to allow souls to reincarnate and undergo soul training and is not complete in itself.

In modern society, however, people try to decide their happiness or unhappiness or determine which country is happy or unhappy within the boundaries of this earthly world only. In this trend, people have forgotten to consider what is justice from the perspective of the world beyond this one—namely, the heavenly world—or of the Supreme Being called God or Buddha. The idea that God's justice must be realized in this world is missing in modern society.

That is why people think that justice is the law made by the parliament within a country and that it is the treaties, international law, and pacts reached through negotiations between countries. Then, this will ultimately mean that international justice is backed by military power, and it automatically makes a country with weak military power unable to stand against a country with strong military power.

Taking these things into consideration, even if we promote peace through freedom of speech or expression, for example, we will not be able to win against a military power that tries to oppress us.

Looking at the hierarchy of the heavenly world, it is natural to have fewer people toward the top in an autocratic style as well. But when a human on earth tries to take the place of God and rule over humanity, they are apt to adopt ideas that would prioritize their own profit at the cost of others.

In addition, an increasing number of people will start thinking, "The strong will win, and the weak will lose. The dog-eat-dog system rules this world." In the world of nature, this is a matter of course. However, you must deeply consider whether it is right for human beings to have this idea in this world, which is a training ground for souls.

The danger that the system of
reincarnation might stop

What worries me the most now is this: The population of this world has inflated to eight billion people, and all these people will leave this world sooner or later. But the majority of them will depart without even knowing about heaven and hell. Should that be allowed?

You must also know that, in principle, the machines and gadgets that people depend on in this earthly world do not exist in the Spirit World. All that exists is your spiritual thinking and action. In other words, your thought is your action.

Once you enter the other world, your technology-dependent life or lifestyle, or the way the world on earth works around machines, will all be gone. There are many people who were not taught about what a soul is capable of doing on its own in a world without machines, and they are now falling into the world of darkness.

In a sense, we are almost reaching a limit. If more than half of all human souls end up in hell, the values of good and evil on Earth can flip, just as how the majority rule in the democratic way of thinking works.

What would happen as a result? The outcome would be extremely severe. It means the number of people who would listen to the voice of devils would surpass those who listen to the voice of God.

This phenomenal world of the third dimension is much closer to hell than to heaven. That is because hell was initially formed when souls from heaven grew too accustomed to the physical vibrations of the earthly world and could only live in an earthly way in the other world.

The number of these souls is rapidly increasing, and this should not be neglected. Historically, a number of saviors were sent down to earth to dissolve hell, along with many archangels, angels, tathagatas, and bodhisattvas to support them. However, they are buried under freedom of speech and freedom of thought and are left unnoticed. In this way, people have become unable to tell what is right and what is wrong.

What is worse, these days, more and more people prefer the wrong values; those who have taught wrong ideologies are given worldly status and fame, whereas those who have taught the right things are not given worldly recognition. Many cases like this have been occurring.

Therefore, there will come a point when humanity will need to repent. Humanity is already experiencing times of tribulation, and this will continue for some time.

By "some time," I do not mean an indefinite time; I foresee that within these 20–30 years at the most, the general direction of humanity will be decided.

If this world is ruled by the values opposite to those of heaven or God and Buddha and is directly connected to hell, the time will come when Earth Consciousness and the Will of God and Buddha must halt the soul training on earth.

In other words, the system of reincarnation on earth could halt for some time to purify the earth.

How will it stop? It will stop through all kinds of incidents that you can think of. Many things will continuously happen and make it very difficult for humans to live.

I am sure humans on earth are slowly coming to realize this. Pandemics, war, food shortages, abnormally hot or cold weather, typhoons, floods, and many other unknown phenomena might suddenly strike humanity.

It is true that the workings of hell are affecting this Phenomenal World, but one thing I must tell you now is that hell itself is being intruded upon by beings from the outside of Earth. Unfortunately, this matter is far beyond human understanding.

Humans still do not even know whether extraterrestrial beings exist or not. From the perspective of the entire universe and humanoid aliens, Earth is still at an extremely low level in recognizing or understanding outer space. There has been influences and intervention from outer space. Yet, I have to say Earthlings are incredibly ignorant and vulnerable to this fact.

I mean that some extraterrestrial beings are actually exercising their power of influence over the leaders on

Earth. Of course, some of them are giving positive influence; but others are giving negative influence, and this power is escalating. It is not only the power of Earth-born devils in hell that affects people but also the dark power of the universe.

So the next issue is this: How should we deter this dark power? In some countries, their leaders and people have become mediums of the dark power of the universe. In other words, such extraterrestrial beings of the dark have "walked-in" to them and are using them to realize their ideals on earth.

One method to deter this is to put these countries in a critical situation and make their regimes collapse. This could be one option, but that alone will not resolve the problem. Even if such regimes were to collapse in this world, people of those regimes will only shift their work over to the world of hell after death. This will increase the forces of hell, resulting in a power struggle of hell vs. heaven. If the forces of hell grow too large, heaven and hell will lose their power balance.

Take the word *forgiveness*, for example. Some people may take it to mean that you must forgive everyone no matter what evil, crime, or action they have committed or no matter what kinds of evil thoughts they have. But according to this idea, any evil person can go to heaven, not hell, and consequently, heaven itself will turn into hell.

Just imagine what it would be like if the police and gangs were jumbled or if they switched positions. Historically, this occasionally happened in a country ruled by dictators.

This will result in a society that cares little about people's happiness. If Earth reaches that point, the whole system of reincarnation will most likely collapse.

When this happens, souls that are meant to suffer, be punished or receive treatment in hell will no longer go through such processes. Instead, after they die, these souls will remain on earth and go around possessing and manipulating the physical bodies of living human beings. In the case of this, the system of reincarnation will break down, and some souls will become parasites that forever inhabit physical bodies. When the physical body of a person they are attached to perish, they will move on to the next person. Then, the souls of the bodies under possession will also turn into malicious spirits and start possessing other people's bodies.

At this level, it will become extremely difficult to reincarnate on earth from the heavenly world.

The "world emperor" might appear and annihilate ethnicities and nations that believe in God or Buddha

The most ideal way is to spread Buddha's Truth that we currently teach to the whole world and have everyone in the world understand it and make it their guidelines to live by.

But population-wise, this will not be so easy to accomplish.

From now on, the heavenly world will send down numerous warnings, but I am concerned that most people will not notice even then. They will most probably dismiss them as mere coincidences or natural phenomena.

In addition, I fear that more and more people will come to think, "The police and the military in this world have real power. So those who can take command of the police or military at will are the most powerful ones; they are the living gods of the modern world."

But God is not just kind; God also has a strict aspect in Him. God will make those who are wrong pay the price accordingly.

For example, in the past, two atomic bombs were dropped on Japan, but only the Japanese and a small group of sympathetic people remember this. Since other countries have not suffered from them, there could be a dropping of an atomic or hydrogen bomb on yet another country before the reduction of nuclear weapons is realized. Unfortunately, it seems that people cannot understand others' pain, although they can feel their own. So I think this can soon happen.

When there is a country that has nuclear weapons and a country that does not, what can ultimately happen is that the former can tell the latter, "If you don't obey us, we'll launch nuclear attacks and exterminate you." If this happens, then the country without nuclear weapons will only have two options: Either to become complete slaves or to perish.

Even in the past, when nuclear weapons did not exist, Asia and South America were ruled by the great powers of the West. Like those times, some countries might have to face a situation where they have to choose between being colonized and becoming extinct.

Now that we have entered the space age, there might also be attacks from outer space in the near future, which may seriously damage the conditions that are allowing humans to live on earth.

Therefore, you must start by knowing the facts and understanding the current situation. We must not allow this planet to become devils' planet.

By "devils' planet," I mean Earth that is ruled by evil.

For example, if a gang boss were the chief of police, the town or city mayor, the prefectural governor, or the prime minister, the people living during his time would go through tremendous suffering. Even worse, if he were not a gang boss but a psychopath, then things would be much crueler.

There were actually many eras in the past when leaders completely oppressed or massacred the people who stood against them, who would show any sign of rebellion, or who held anti-regime ideology. It happened again and again. However, due to the restrictions of the age, such incidents were limited to each region most of the time. But just imagine what it would be like if something similar to the Nazi persecution of the Jews were to occur on a global scale. That would be truly horrifying.

If a so-called world emperor were to appear and say, "From now on, any person, ethnic group, or country with faith in God and Buddha will be destroyed," people would no longer have faith.

Thus, we have now entered an age when humans are controlled by the arms and weapons they themselves have made. It is also an age when computer systems that humans have created are watching over them, as if they are ants being watched and individually controlled.

3

Begin the Spiritual Fight to Regain Human Nature

Establishing El Cantare Belief all over the world in this modern age

So here is my message: First, regain human nature. It is important that you regain the true mission you should naturally have as a human being.

It is a part of human instinct to have faith. Humans are different from tiny creatures such as ants; humans are humans precisely because they have the instinct to believe that God and Buddha exist. This is the precondition of human souls.

It comes from the Truth that humans were originally divided from a greater light; the souls of people living in this world are fragments of bigger souls, and these bigger souls are fragments of yet even larger souls, and so on. The light that dwells within human beings is originally a particle of God's Light or Buddha's Soul. Therefore, humans must not degrade themselves as mere "dust." This is their natural duty.

That is why we must now begin our spiritual fight.

In particular, people in countries that are about to wage war might believe they are just following their leaders, but they need to know that their leaders are actually starting to be manipulated by the "messengers of darkness" that have come from outer space. These beings adopt different approaches; they might spiritually possess the leaders or send inspiration, or they might be "walking in" to the leaders' physical bodies on earth while their real body remains in a spaceship. There are increasing numbers of people who are now coming under the control of dark beings in these ways.

The day of the final battle for it is approaching; sadly, the forces of light are still very weak. I am filled with sadness to see that the forces of evil are expanding so quickly beneath our feet like an underground stem.

The book by Nietzsche in which he wrote, "God is dead," only sold 40-100 copies in its first edition; Nietzsche himself paid to get it published. But before long, the mass media and education were used as means to spread his ideology, and it has since permeated in different forms throughout the world. If philosophy and science are developed based on the premise that "God is dead," all other academic structures will follow suit.

If the earthly world becomes like this and reaches a point when we can no longer turn the situation around through ideological warfare, there is a possibility that humanity will become extinct. That is what happened to the ancient continents of Atlantis, Mu, and Lemuria (Ramudia).

Ultimately, things may go as far as that. It occurred only about 10,000 years ago, and it may well happen now.

The day will come unexpectedly. It will come all of a sudden, without giving any time for humanity to prepare for it. So I say to you: With all your might, please do as much as you can in your given time.

What is it that I want you to do? Let me state it clearly.

Please firmly establish El Cantare Belief, now, in this modern age. Make sure to establish El Cantare Belief not only in Japan but also across the world.

It means to believe that the being now called "El Cantare" was Alpha—the Creator of Earth—and Elohim—the One who established justice in this world—and that now, He is trying to fight against the final crisis of Earth. Please establish this faith.

Explore Right Mind and practice the modern Fourfold Path

Living with this faith is, put simply, the *Exploration of Right Mind*. I have now condensed it into the *modern Fourfold Path*, which comprises love, wisdom, self-reflection, and progress.

1) Love—Make a paradigm shift from "taking love" to "giving love"

First is the teaching of *love*. The majority of people misunderstand love. An increasing number of people simply believe that love is something to take or is given by others. This idea is prevalent in communist countries as well—often in the economic sense. They believe, "The have-nots have the right to exploit the haves by taking from them."

But this way of thinking is wrong. Humans are born into this world for the purpose of spiritually developing themselves by making efforts and achieving something of value. That is why it is not good to take what other people have earned through hard work when you yourself did nothing or to create a system that allows you to do so. Creating such a system can also lead to the corruption of individuals.

Another example of the misunderstanding of love is the social welfarism found in liberal societies. I will not go as far as to deny that this is one of the useful systems that humanity invented, but in some cases, it has merely been used as a replacement for communism in dissolving people's dissatisfaction and complaints. As a result, it can cause a nation to go bankrupt and collapse on its own without God or Buddha having to use their power.

In Japan, too, the government continues to spend twice as much as the tax its citizens pay. This indicates that the country will go bankrupt at some point in time. The same can be said of the United States and most members of the EU; some poor countries in Asia and Africa have already gone through bankruptcy.

Here is the answer to this problem: You must have an "It's enough" mind and think about how to live within your income.

It is important to make a paradigm shift regarding love: From *taking love* to *giving love*. Giving love is the power of God or Buddha that has been allowing humanity to live. Humans must also take on a role and practice a kind of love that indiscriminately sheds light, just like the sun.

2) Wisdom—Study Buddha's Truth to develop your soul

What, then, is *wisdom* in the Fourfold Path of love, wisdom, self-reflection, and progress? It means Buddha's Truth. Even if you gain knowledge in this world, your soul will not develop unless that knowledge is backed by the true perspective of the world, the spiritual truth, or the teachings of God and Buddha.

I must say it is absolutely wrong to think that, "God is dead," "It's all about materialism," or "Convenience in this world is the best thing. That is what happiness is." If humanity does not even know where they came from and where they will go, they are the same as people standing on the platform of a station without knowing why they are there. In reality, you are waiting for the next train to get somewhere. Not knowing where you came from and where you are going means you have forgotten who you are.

3) Self-reflection—Look back on your thoughts and actions, the sins you committed, and polish your mind

Next is *self-reflection*.

Human souls sometimes fall to hell. When you have lived your life in a way that goes against Buddha's Truth, you will fall to hell.

At that time, however, you must not become rebellious in vain and join the force that defies God. You yourself must reflect on your thoughts and actions, the sins you have committed, and repent. Through self-reflection, you can polish your mind and return to the heavenly world. You are given this ability.

So please regain this power and make it the basis for your learning as you live.

4) Progress—Create utopia where those who have accumulated virtue can lead many people

Last is *progress*, which includes "creating utopia."

Creating utopia is mentioned in various ideologies, but you must be able to strictly distinguish utopia from dystopia. Do not think that the world similar to the one portrayed in George Orwell's *1984* or *Animal Farm* is utopia. You must aim to create a country and society where those who have accumulated virtue through spiritual training on earth can lead many people.

Needless to say, it is unforgivable for any leader to establish power by skillfully lying or using money, status, or fame to instigate people. It is out of the question for anyone to control society in the way that they like by making up a conspiracy. What is more, we should not allow people to use the mass media to misguide the public into believing wrong information and push everyone into the sea—such a thing should never happen.

A true utopian society must be one that can harmonize with the heavenly world.

I am very saddened to see how excessive doubt and suspicion are taking over the mass media as it grows powerful.

Another concern is that in the modern democratic society, how much knowledge you have gained in this world has become something that represents your status. The amount of knowledge acquired has replaced the class system. This has become the trend nowadays. However, "becoming knowledgeable" does not necessarily mean "becoming wise."

From what you have learned, pick out the real knowledge that contains diamond-like brilliance, use it in what you experience as "life's training," and transform it into wisdom. That is important.

Today, however, things are different. One's educational background, such as mere grades and school rankings, is being used to pick out individuals to be put in leading positions. Based on such records, these chosen individuals act as if they are born-to-be aristocrats and look down on others, rule others, or give others orders. Unfortunately, this is not a heavenly attitude but a mere delusion.

Strive to create a better society by practicing the Fourfold Path

Be open-minded and ask yourself,
"Am I living with God's Will as my own?"
"Am I living with God's Wisdom as my own?"
People who make efforts
By humbly reflecting on themselves on these points
Should be the ones who accumulate a lot of wisdom
And lead others.
With this in mind,
You must also be overflowing with love,
Recognize your own mistakes,
Encourage each other to study the Truth,
And put in the effort to create a better society.
The direction you should aim at
Is not materialism or scientism
That focuses solely on this world.

No matter how much science has advanced,
It still cannot unveil the mystery of life.
Why do larvae born from small eggs in the soil
Come out to the surface
And turn into beetles or stag beetles?
Science cannot even answer that.

Why do human bodies develop
In the way that they do?
Why does each organ inside our bodies
Function in its own way?
Why does the brain system carry all kinds of functions
When we didn't make it ourselves?
We have now discovered and researched what DNA is,
But why does it exist in the first place?
Humanity cannot answer these questions.
Some deluded scientists say that DNA is the soul itself.
They even believe,
"The passing down of DNA
From parents to children to grandchildren
Is the reincarnation of the soul."
But I must say that this is nothing but
A modern-day expression of religious ignorance.

4

My Hope Is to Maintain Earth as the Training Ground for Souls

Utopia on earth
—The world of *Truth*, *Goodness*, and *Beauty*

My hope is, of course, to maintain Earth
As the place for many souls to reincarnate
And undergo spiritual training in their future lives too.
I would also like many people to understand that
In the eyes of space beings,
This Earth is a very much preferred
Training ground for souls.

We must return to the origin of education
And reform it completely to how it should be.
If possible, we must establish
The world of goodness through all our activities.
Creating utopia on earth is, in other words,
To establish the world of Truth, Goodness, and Beauty—
The true world, the good world, and the beautiful world.
Yet this utopia must not be the kind of utopia
That makes souls grow attached

To the earthly world forever.
One day, you will leave your physical body
And enter another world where you do not eat
Or cannot even hold hands with another person.
You will move on to such an illusion-like world,
But that is the real world.
Humans must become wise enough
To be able to understand this.

Each of you must accomplish your grand mission —Save the mind of each person

Now, I'm deeply concerned that
Hell is increasing its territory and how evil is spreading
In the minds of people living in this earthly world.
I want people to be strong.
The real world is the invisible world,
And the visible world is the temporary world.
Those who have a foothold in this world
Might find it difficult to understand this,
But I hope you will study this paradoxical Truth:
Those who can see in this world are actually blind,
While those who can see what is not of this world
Can truly see.

If you can grasp this, and only this,
You will be able to understand
What lies at the core of all religions and its meaning.
All suffering or sadness in this world
Are there for the happiness of your future lives.
So even if you experience
Suffering and sadness in this world,
You must not regard them as your life itself.
Experience is just an experience—
Only when you learn from it,
The truth shall shed its light.
Please don't forget this.

From now on, we will be entering the age
Where we fight for the Truth.
The state that the world is in now is
Still very far from how I wish it to be.
I don't know how much I can bear.
But the crisis is drawing near;
In fact, it is already happening now.
Please know that we are running through a crisis now.

Uphold what is truly sacred as sacred
And disregard what is not.
I hope you will live by distinguishing them apart.

This concludes what I want to say for this chapter,
"A Message from Savior."
Please try to understand my true intention.
The many books of Happy Science
Will help you understand this.
I sincerely pray from my heart
That each one of you will fulfill your great mission—
To save the mind of each person, one by one.

Afterword

"You're still talking about the Special Judge of Hell, King Yama, and the Red Punisher even in this modern age? Give me a break." I'm sure many people will think this way. They would say, "Such figures are from *Japanese Folk Tales*. They aren't mentioned in school textbooks nor do they come up in entrance exams. Shakyamuni Buddha was prehistory; Jesus was a good-for-nothing son of a carpenter. Socrates was a critic of majority rule who abused the name of God.

"How can I possibly believe that Ame-no-Mioya-Gami, Japanese Father God, descended on Mount Fuji from the Andromeda Galaxy, 30,000 years ago, to create the Japanese race?"

There are others that say, "What's wrong with men and women having sex as they like? We are no different from dogs."

"Religion is all about brainwashing. It's all spiritual fraud."

No angels can be found among journalists who say such things. Even lawyers would go down to hell. Even the guy who was given a state funeral in his honor had his tongue yanked out by Yama for lying.

Those who are considered "great" in this world will be "small," whereas those who are considered "small" in this world will be "great." Regardless of your education, career, or the number of awards or medals you received, you are bound to go to hell if you don't know about the good and evil of the mind.

Ryuho Okawa
Master & CEO of Happy Science Group
November 2022

TRANSLATOR'S NOTES

1 The Special Judge of Hell in Buddhism and Hinduism. Recently, Happy Science has revealed that Yamas exist in the Spirit World of several countries including Japan.

2 Shinran (1173–1263)
Japanese Buddhist monk and the founder of the True Pure Land School of Buddhism.

- Chapter One -

Introduction to Hell

Japanese title: *Jigoku Nyumon*
Lecture given on July 24, 2022
at the Special Lecture Hall, Happy Science, Japan

- Chapter Two -

The Laws of Hell

Japanese title: *Jigoku no Ho*
Lecture given on July 25, 2022
at the Special Lecture Hall, Happy Science, Japan

- Chapter Three -

Curses, Spells, and Possession

Japanese title: *Noroi to Hyo-i*
Lecture given on August 1, 2022
at the Special Lecture Hall, Happy Science, Japan

- Chapter Four -

The Fight against Devils

Japanese title: *Akuma to no Tatakai*
Lecture given on August 3, 2022
at the Special Lecture Hall, Happy Science, Japan

- Chapter Five -

A Message from Savior

Japanese title: *Kyuseishu kara no Message*
Lecture given on August 6, 2022
at the Special Lecture Hall, Happy Science, Japan

For a deeper understanding of The Laws of Hell,
see other books below by Ryuho Okawa:

The Laws of the Sun [New York, IRH Press, 2018]

The Golden Laws [Tokyo, HS Press, 2015]

The Nine Dimensions [New York, IRH Press, 2012]

The Laws of Secret [New York, IRH Press, 2021]

The Real Exorcist [New York, IRH Press, 2020]

The Spiritual Truth About Curses and Spells [Tokyo, HS Press, 2022]

The Unknown Stigma 1 <The Mystery> [New York, IRH Press, 2022]

ABOUT THE AUTHOR

Founder and CEO of Happy Science Group.

Ryuho Okawa was born on July 7th 1956, in Tokushima, Japan. After graduating from the University of Tokyo with a law degree, he joined a Tokyo-based trading house. While working at its New York headquarters, he studied international finance at the Graduate Center of the City University of New York. In 1981, he attained Great Enlightenment and became aware that he is El Cantare with a mission to bring salvation to all humankind.

In 1986, he established Happy Science. It now has members in 168 countries across the world, with more than 700 branches and temples as well as 10,000 missionary houses around the world.

He has given over 3,450 lectures (of which more than 150 are in English) and published over 3,100 books (of which more than 600 are Spiritual Interview Series), and many are translated into 41 languages. Along with *The Laws of the Sun* and *The Laws of Hell*, many of the books have become best sellers or million sellers. To date, Happy Science has produced 27 movies. The original story and original concept were given by the Executive Producer Ryuho Okawa. He has also composed music and written lyrics of over 450 pieces.

Moreover, he is the Founder of Happy Science University and Happy Science Academy (Junior and Senior High School), Founder and President of the Happiness Realization Party, Founder and Honorary Headmaster of Happy Science Institute of Government and Management, Founder of IRH Press Co., Ltd., and the Chairperson of NEW STAR PRODUCTION Co., Ltd. and ARI Production Co., Ltd.

WHAT IS EL CANTARE?

El Cantare means "the Light of the Earth," and is the Supreme God of the Earth who has been guiding humankind since the beginning of Genesis. He is whom Jesus called Father and Muhammad called Allah, and is *Ame-no-Mioya-Gami*, Japanese Father God. Different parts of El Cantare's core consciousness have descended to Earth in the past, once as Alpha and another as Elohim. His branch spirits, such as Shakyamuni Buddha and Hermes, have descended to Earth many times and helped to flourish many civilizations. To unite various religions and to integrate various fields of study in order to build a new civilization on Earth, a part of the core consciousness has descended to Earth as Master Ryuho Okawa.

Alpha is a part of the core consciousness of El Cantare who descended to Earth around 330 million years ago. Alpha preached Earth's Truths to harmonize and unify Earth-born humans and space people who came from other planets.

Elohim is a part of the core consciousness of El Cantare who descended to Earth around 150 million years ago. He gave wisdom, mainly on the differences of light and darkness, good and evil.

Ame-no-Mioya-Gami (Japanese Father God) is the Creator God and the Father God who appears in the ancient literature, *Hotsuma Tsutae*. It is believed that He descended on the foothills of Mt. Fuji about 30,000 years ago and built the Fuji dynasty, which is the root of the Japanese civilization. With justice as the central pillar, Ame-no-Mioya-Gami's teachings spread to ancient civilizations of other countries in the world.

Shakyamuni Buddha was born as a prince into the Shakya Clan in India around 2,600 years ago. When he was 29 years old, he renounced the world and sought enlightenment. He later attained Great Enlightenment and founded Buddhism.

Hermes is one of the 12 Olympian gods in Greek mythology, but the spiritual Truth is that he taught the teachings of love and progress around 4,300 years ago that became the origin of the current Western civilization. He is a hero that truly existed.

Ophealis was born in Greece around 6,500 years ago and was the leader who took an expedition to as far as Egypt. He is the God of miracles, prosperity, and arts, and is known as Osiris in the Egyptian mythology.

Rient Arl Croud was born as a king of the ancient Incan Empire around 7,000 years ago and taught about the mysteries of the mind. In the heavenly world, he is responsible for the interactions that take place between various planets.

Thoth was an almighty leader who built the golden age of the Atlantic civilization around 12,000 years ago. In the Egyptian mythology, he is known as god Thoth.

Ra Mu was a leader who built the golden age of the civilization of Mu around 17,000 years ago. As a religious leader and a politician, he ruled by uniting religion and politics.

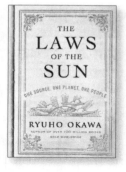

The Laws of the Sun

One Source, One Planet, One People

Paperback • 288 pages • $15.95
ISBN: 978-1-942125-43-3 (Oct. 15, 2018)

Imagine if you could ask God why he created this world and what spiritual laws he used to shape us—and everything around us. In *The Laws of the Sun*, Ryuho Okawa outlines these laws of the universe and provides a road map for living one's life with greater purpose and meaning.

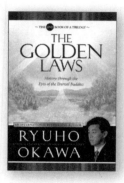

The Golden Laws

History through the Eyes of the Eternal Buddha

E-book • 204 pages • $13.99
ISBN: 978-1-941779-82-8 (Sep. 24, 2015)

Throughout history, Great Guiding Spirits of Light have been present on Earth in both the East and the West at crucial points in human history to further our spiritual development. *The Golden Laws* reveals how Divine Plan has been unfolding on Earth, and outlines 5,000 years of the secret history of humankind.

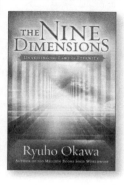

The Nine Dimensions

Unveiling the Laws of Eternity

Paperback • 168 pages • $15.95
ISBN: 978-0-982698-56-3 (Feb. 16, 2012)

This book is a window into the mind of our loving God. When the religions and cultures of the world discover the truth of their common spiritual origin, they will be inspired to accept their differences, come together under faith in God, and build an era of harmony and peaceful progress on Earth.

LAWS SERIES

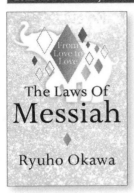

The 28th Laws Series

The Laws Of Messiah

From Love to Love

Paperback • 248 pages • $16.95
ISBN: 978-1-942125-90-7 (Jan. 31, 2022)

"What is Messiah?" This book carries an important message of love and guidance to people living now from the Modern-Day Messiah or the Modern-Day Savior. It also reveals the secret of Shambhala, the spiritual center of Earth, as well as the truth that this spiritual center is currently in danger of perishing and what we can do to protect this sacred place.

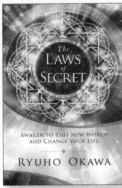

The 27th Laws Series

The Laws of Secret

Awaken to This New World
and Change Your Life

Paperback • 248 pages • $16.95
ISBN:978-1-942125-81-5 (Apr. 20, 2021)

Our physical world coexists with the multi-dimensional spirit world and we are constantly interacting with some kind of spiritual energy, whether positive or negative, without consciously realizing it. This book reveals how our lives are affected by invisible influences, including the spiritual reasons behind influenza, the novel coronavirus infection, and other illnesses. The new view of the world in this book will inspire you to change your life in a better direction, and to become someone who can give hope and courage to others in this age of confusion.

LEARN THE SPIRITUAL TRUTH AND AVOID GOING TO HELL

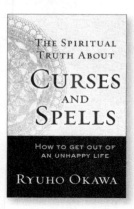

The Spiritual Truth About Curses and Spells

How to Get Out of an Unhappy Life

Paperback • 140 pages • $14.95
ISBN: 978-8-88737-062-0 (Sep. 28, 2022)

Curses occur in daily life; this is the Spiritual Truth. Our feelings of jealousy and anger can be transmitted as thoughts of curses and cause harm to others, or they can be repelled back to us and bring us misfortune. This book teaches you the method to protect yourself from such curses and stop the cursing that brings unhappiness to yourself and others.

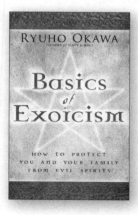

Basics of Exorcism

How to Protect You and Your Family from Evil Spirits

Paperback • 130 pages • $14.95
ISBN: 978-1-941779-34-7 (Jan. 6, 2015)

No matter how much time progresses, demons are real. Spiritual screen against curses – the truth of exorcism as told by the author who possesses the six great supernatural powers – The essence of exorcism as a result of more than 5,000 rounds of exorcist experience!

The Real Exorcist

Attain Wisdom to Conquer Evil

Paperback • 208 pages • $16.95
ISBN:978-1-942125-67-9 (Jun. 15, 2020)

This is a profound spiritual text backed by the author's nearly 40 years of real-life experience with spiritual phenomena. In it, Okawa teaches how we may discern and overcome our negative tendencies, by acquiring the right knowledge, mindset and lifestyle.

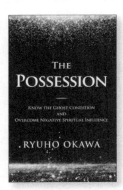

The Possession

Know the Ghost Condition and Overcome Negative Spiritual Influence

Paperback • 114 pages • $14.95
ISBN: 978-1-943869-66-4 (Feb. 11, 2020)

Possession is neither an exceptional occurrence nor unscientific superstition; it's a phenomenon, based on spiritual principles, that is still quite common in the modern society. Through this book, you can find the way to change your own mind and free yourself from possession, and the way to exorcise devils by relying on the power of angels and God.

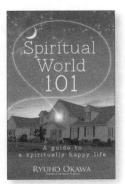

Spiritual World 101

A Guide to a Spiritually Happy Life

Paperback • 184 pages • $14.95
ISBN: 978-1-941779-43-9 (Feb. 10, 2015)

This book is a spiritual guidebook that will answer all your questions about the spiritual world, with illustrations and diagrams explaining about your guardian spirit and the secrets of God and Buddha. By reading this book, you will be able to understand the true meaning of life and find happiness in everyday life.

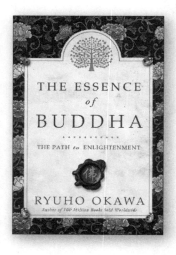

The Essence of Buddha

The Path to Enlightenment

Paperback • 208 pages • $14.95
ISBN: 978-1-942125-06-8 (Oct. 1, 2016)

In this book, Ryuho Okawa imparts in simple and accessible language his wisdom about the essence of Shakyamuni Buddha's philosophy of life and enlightenment–teachings that have been inspiring people all over the world for over 2,500 years. By offering a new perspective on core Buddhist thoughts that have long been cloaked in mystique, Okawa brings these teachings to life for modern people. *The Essence of Buddha* distills a way of life that anyone can practice to achieve a life of self-growth, compassionate living, and true happiness.

The Challenge of Enlightenment

Now, Here, the New Dharma Wheel Turns

Paperback • 380 pages • $17.95
ISBN: 978-1-942125-92-1 (Dec. 20, 2022)

Buddha's teachings, a reflection of his eternal wisdom, are like a bamboo pole used to change the course of your boat in the rapid stream of the great river called life. By reading this book, your mind becomes clearer, learns to savor inner peace, and it will empower you to make profound life improvements.

The Rebirth of Buddha

My Eternal Disciples, Hear My Words

Paperback • 280 pages • $17.95
ISBN: 978-1-942125-95-2 (Jul. 15, 2022)

These are the messages of Buddha who has returned to this modern age as promised to His eternal beloved disciples. They are in simple words and poetic style, yet contain profound messages. Once you start reading these passages, your soul will be replenished as the plant absorbs the water, and you will remember why you chose this era to be born into with Buddha. Listen to the voices of your Eternal Master and awaken to your calling.

A New Genre of Spiritual Mystery Novels
- The Unknown Stigma Trilogy -

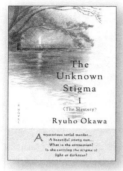

The Unknown Stigma 1 <The Mystery>

Hardcover • 192 pages • $17.95
ISBN: 978-1-942125-28-0

The first spiritual mystery novel by Ryuho Okawa. It happened one early summer afternoon, in a densely wooded park in Tokyo: following a loud scream of a young woman, the alleged victim was found lying with his eyes rolled back and foaming at the mouth. But there was no sign of forced trauma, nor even a drop of blood. Then, similar murder cases continued one after another without any clues. Later, this mysterious serial murder case leads back to a young Catholic nun...

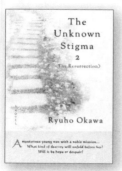

The Unknown Stigma 2 <The Resurrection>

Hardcover • 180 pages • $17.95
ISBN: 978-1-942125-31-0

A sequel to *The Unknown Stigma 1 <The Mystery>* by Ryuho Okawa. After an extraordinary spiritual experience, a young, mysterious Catholic nun is now endowed with a new, noble mission. What kind of destiny will she face? Will it be hope or despair that awaits her? The story develops into a turn of events that no one could ever have anticipated. Are you ready to embrace its shocking ending?

The Unknown Stigma 3 <The Universe>

Hardcover • 184 pages • $17.95
ISBN: 978-1-958655-00-9

In this astonishing sequel to the first two installments of *The Unknown Stigma*, the protagonist journeys through the universe and encounters a mystical world unknown to humankind. Discover what awaits her beyond this mysterious world.

OTHER RECOMMENDED TITLES

The Ten Principles from El Cantare Volume I
Ryuho Okawa's First Lectures on His Basic Teachings

The Ten Principles from El Cantare Volume II
Ryuho Okawa's First Lectures on His Wish to Save the World

The New Resurrection
My Miraculous Story of Overcoming Illness and Death

Twiceborn
My Early Thoughts that Revealed My True Mission

The Power of Basics
Introduction to Modern Zen Life
of Calm, Spirituality and Success

The True Eightfold Path
Guideposts for Self-Innovation

Developmental Stages of Love - The Original Theory
Philosophy of Love in My Youth

Rojin, Buddha's Mystical Power
Its Ultimate Attainment in Today's World

My Journey Through the Spirit World
A True Account of My Experiences of the Hereafter

For a complete list of books, visit okawabooks.com

"The True Words Spoken By Buddha"

This is one of the greatest gospels for humankind; this sutra, which is the English version of Happy Science's basic sutra, was written directly in English by Master Ryuho Okawa.

Available to Happy Science members. You may receive it at your nearest Happy Science location. See pp.262-263.

MUSIC BY RYUHO OKAWA

ABOUT HAPPY SCIENCE

Happy Science is a global movement that empowers individuals to find purpose and spiritual happiness and to share that happiness with their families, societies, and the world. With more than 12 million members around the world, Happy Science aims to increase awareness of spiritual truths and expand our capacity for love, compassion, and joy so that together we can create the kind of world we all wish to live in.

Activities at Happy Science are based on the Principles of Happiness (Love, Wisdom, Self-Reflection, and Progress). These principles embrace worldwide philosophies and beliefs, transcending boundaries of culture and religions.

Love teaches us to give ourselves freely without expecting anything in return; it encompasses giving, nurturing, and forgiving.

Wisdom leads us to the insights of spiritual truths, and opens us to the true meaning of life and the Will of God (the universe, the highest power, Buddha).

Self-Reflection brings a mindful, nonjudgmental lens to our thoughts and actions to help us find our truest selves—the essence of our souls—and deepen our connection to the highest power. It helps us attain a clean and peaceful mind and leads us to the right life path.

Progress emphasizes the positive, dynamic aspects of our spiritual growth—actions we can take to manifest and spread happiness around the world. It's a path that not only expands our soul growth, but also furthers the collective potential of the world we live in.

PROGRAMS AND EVENTS

The doors of Happy Science are open to all. We offer a variety of programs and events, including self-exploration and self-growth programs, spiritual seminars, meditation and contemplation sessions, study groups, and book events.

Our programs are designed to:
* Deepen your understanding of your purpose and meaning in life
* Improve your relationships and increase your capacity to love unconditionally
* Attain peace of mind, decrease anxiety and stress, and feel positive
* Gain deeper insights and a broader perspective on the world
* Learn how to overcome life's challenges
  ... and much more.

For more information, visit happy-science.org.

CONTACT INFORMATION

Happy Science is a worldwide organization with branches and temples around the globe. For a comprehensive list, visit the worldwide directory at *happy-science.org*. The following are some of the many Happy Science locations:

UNITED STATES AND CANADA

New York
79 Franklin St., New York, NY 10013, USA
Phone: 1-212-343-7972
Fax: 1-212-343-7973
Email: ny@happy-science.org
Website: happyscience-usa.org

New Jersey
66 Hudson St., #2R, Hoboken, NJ 07030, USA
Phone: 1-201-313-0127
Email: nj@happy-science.org
Website: happyscience-usa.org

Chicago
2300 Barrington Rd., Suite #400, Hoffman Estates, IL 60169, USA
Phone: 1-630-937-3077
Email: chicago@happy-science.org
Website: happyscience-usa.org

Florida
5208 8th St., Zephyrhills, FL 33542, USA
Phone: 1-813-715-0000
Fax: 1-813-715-0010
Email: florida@happy-science.org
Website: happyscience-usa.org

Atlanta
1874 Piedmont Ave., NE Suite 360-C
Atlanta, GA 30324, USA
Phone: 1-404-892-7770
Email: atlanta@happy-science.org
Website: happyscience-usa.org

San Francisco
525 Clinton St. Redwood City, CA 94062, USA
Phone & Fax: 1-650-363-2777
Email: sf@happy-science.org
Website: happyscience-usa.org

Los Angeles
1590 E. Del Mar Blvd., Pasadena, CA 91106, USA
Phone: 1-626-395-7775
Fax: 1-626-395-7776
Email: la@happy-science.org
Website: happyscience-usa.org

Orange County
16541 Gothard St. Suite 104
Huntington Beach, CA 92647
Phone: 1-714-659-1501
Email: oc@happy-science.org
Website: happyscience-usa.org

San Diego
7841 Balboa Ave. Suite #202
San Diego, CA 92111, USA
Phone: 1-626-395-7775
Fax: 1-626-395-7776
E-mail: sandiego@happy-science.org
Website: happyscience-usa.org

Hawaii
Phone: 1-808-591-9772
Fax: 1-808-591-9776
Email: hi@happy-science.org
Website: happyscience-usa.org

Kauai
3343 Kanakolu Street, Suite 5
Lihue, HI 96766, USA
Phone: 1-808-822-7007
Fax: 1-808-822-6007
Email: kauai-hi@happy-science.org
Website: happyscience-usa.org

Toronto
845 The Queensway Etobicoke,
ON M8Z 1N6, Canada
Phone: 1-416-901-3747
Email: toronto@happy-science.org
Website: happy-science.ca

INTERNATIONAL

Tokyo
1-6-7 Togoshi, Shinagawa,
Tokyo, 142-0041, Japan
Phone: 81-3-6384-5770
Fax: 81-3-6384-5776
Email: tokyo@happy-science.org
Website: happy-science.org

London
3 Margaret St.London,
W1W 8RE United Kingdom
Phone: 44-20-7323-9255
Fax: 44-20-7323-9344
Email: eu@happy-science.org
Website: www.happyscience-uk.org

Sydney
516 Pacific Highway, Lane Cove North,
2066 NSW, Australia
Phone: 61-2-9411-2877
Fax: 61-2-9411-2822
Email: sydney@happy-science.org

Sao Paulo
Rua. Domingos de Morais 1154,
Vila Mariana, Sao Paulo SP
CEP 04010-100, Brazil
Phone: 55-11-5088-3800
Email: sp@happy-science.org
Website: happyscience.com.br

Jundiai
Rua Congo, 447, Jd. Bonfiglioli
Jundiai-CEP, 13207-340, Brazil
Phone: 55-11-4587-5952
Email: jundiai@happy-science.org

Vancouver
#201-2607 East 49th Avenue,
Vancouver, BC, V5S 1J9, Canada
Phone: 1-604-437-7735
Fax: 1-604-437-7764
Email: vancouver@happy-science.org
Website: happy-science.ca

Seoul
74, Sadang-ro 27-gil, Dongjak-gu,
Seoul, Korea
Phone: 82-2-3478-8777
Fax: 82-2-3478-9777
Email: korea@happy-science.org

Taipei
No. 89, Lane 155, Dunhua N. Road,
Songshan District, Taipei City 105, Taiwan
Phone: 886-2-2719-9377
Fax: 886-2-2719-5570
Email: taiwan@happy-science.org

Kuala Lumpur
No 22A, Block 2, Jalil Link Jalan Jalil Jaya 2,
Bukit Jalil 57000,
Kuala Lumpur, Malaysia
Phone: 60-3-8998-7877
Fax: 60-3-8998-7977
Email: malaysia@happy-science.org
Website: happyscience.org.my

Kathmandu
Kathmandu Metropolitan City,
Ward No. 15, Ring Road, Kimdol,
Sitapaila Kathmandu, Nepal
Phone: 977-1-537-2931
Email: nepal@happy-science.org

Kampala
Plot 877 Rubaga Road, Kampala
P.O. Box 34130 Kampala, Uganda
Email: uganda@happy-science.org

ABOUT IRH PRESS USA

IRH Press USA Inc. was founded in 2013 as an affiliated firm of IRH Press Co., Ltd. Based in New York, the press publishes books in various categories including spirituality, religion, and self-improvement and publishes books by Ryuho Okawa, the author of over 100 million books sold worldwide. For more information, visit okawabooks.com.

Follow us on:

f Facebook: Okawa Books **◎** Instagram: OkawaBooks
▶ Youtube: Okawa Books **🐦** Twitter: Okawa Books
𝓟 Pinterest: Okawa Books **g** Goodreads: Ryuho Okawa

———— **NEWSLETTER** ————

To receive book related news, promotions and events, please subscribe to our newsletter below.

& eepurl.com/bsMeJj

———— **AUDIO / VISUAL MEDIA** ————

YOUTUBE   **PODCAST**

Introduction of Ryuho Okawa's titles; topics ranging from self-help, current affairs, spirituality, religion, and the universe.